TRADING STRATEGIES
FOR DIRECT ACCESS TRADING

THE DIRECT ACCESS TRADER SERIES

- *Understanding Direct Access Trading*
  by Rafael Romeu

- *Tools for the Direct Access Trader*
  by Alicia Abell

- *Mastering Direct Access Fundamentals*
  by Jonathan Aspatore with Dan Bress

- *Direct Access Execution*
  by Simit Patel

- *Trading Strategies for Direct Access Trading*
  by Robert Sales

- *Technical Analysis for Direct Access Trading*
  by Rafael Romeu and Umar Serajuddin

TRADING STRATEGIES FOR DIRECT ACCESS TRADING

Making the Most Out of Your Capital

Robert Sales

McGraw-Hill
New York   Chicago   San Francisco
Lisbon   London   Madrid   Mexico City   Milan
New Delhi   San Juan   Seoul   Singapore
Sydney   Toronto

Library of Congress Cataloging-in-Publication Data

Sales, Robert.
    Trading strategies for direct access trading : making the most out of your capital / by
Robert Sales.
        p. cm.
    ISBN 0-07-136392-0
    1. Electronic trading of securities.   2. Risk management.   I. Title.

HG4515.95 .S25 2001
332.64'2'02854678—dc21   2001018696

McGraw-Hill

A Division of The **McGraw·Hill** *Companies*

1 2 3 4 5 6 7 8 9 0   AGM/AGM   0 7 6 5 4 3 2 1

ISBN: 0–07–136392–0

The sponsoring editor for this book was Stephen Isaacs, the editing supervisor was Ruth W. Mannino,
and the production supervisor was Charles Annis. It was set in Times Roman by Binghamton Valley
Composition.

Printed and bound by Quebecor/Martinsburg.

This publication is designed to provide accurate and authoritative information in regard to the subject
matter covered. It is sold with the understanding that neither the author nor the publisher is engaged
in rendering legal, accounting, or other professional service. If legal advice or other expert assistance
is required, the services of a competent professional person should be sought.
—From a Declaration of Principles jointly adopted
by a Committee of the American Bar
Association and a Committee of Publishers

The viewpoints and content expressed by the author are his own and not those of Tradescape.com,
Inc. or any of its affiliated entities, employees, officers, directors, or authorized representatives (the
"Company"). The Company does not endorse any of the content contained herein and has not verified
the accuracy of any of the content. The information is not to be construed as investment advice, and
any reliance on the content as contained herein is at the reader's sole risk and liability.

Brut™ is a trademark of The Brut ECN, RealTick™, of RealTick.com, and NexTrade™, of NexTrade;
E*TRADE® is a registered trademark of E*TRADE, Inc., REDIBook®, of Spear, Leeds & Kellogg,
and Attain®, of ALL-TECH. All other trademarked products mentioned are used in an editorial
fashion only, and to the benefit of the trademark owner, with no intention of infringement of the
trademark. Where such designations appear in this book, they have been printed with initial caps.

This book is printed on recycled, acid-free paper containing a minimum of 50% recycled
de-inked fiber.

*Special thanks to
Jonathan Aspatore, Stephen Isaacs, and Jeffrey Krames
for the opportunity to write this book*

CONTENTS

PREFACE

Trading Strategies for Direct Access Trading is part of the six-book series on direct access trading from McGraw-Hill. The series of books represents the first detailed look at every element of direct access trading for new individuals interested in harnessing the amazing changes occurring in the world's financial markets. All of the books contain a clear and basic approach on how to take advantage of direct access to the markets for your specific level of investing/trading. Direct access trading is for everyone, and in this series of books we show you how to take advantage of it if you only place a couple of trades a year, are starting to get more active in the markets, or even if you want to be a day trader. Take advantage of these revolutionary changes today, and start accessing the markets directly with direct access trading. Good luck!

1

INTRODUCTION AND MARKET SNAPSHOT

The individual investor community, once considered an afterthought in the American equities arena, has become a powerful force. Equipped with direct high-speed access to execution destinations that previously were the exclusive playground of professional broker/dealers and institutional investors, individual investors now compete head-on with the "big boys" to obtain the best prices and achieve the speediest stock executions.

In fact, according to a recent day trading study performed by Bear Stearns, in an era when the two largest stock exchanges in the United States are seemingly breaking volume records every week, full-time day traders who trade on behalf of their own accounts are currently responsible for between 17 and 18 percent of the combined daily volume of the Nasdaq and New York Stock Exchange (NYSE).

Known as *direct access traders,* this small group of investors now sits at the top of the retail stock trading food chain. The direct access trader can view all the best bids and offers for a given stock in real time. More important, he or she can send an order to a specific execution destination and receive nearly instantaneous fills.

In short, thanks to advancements made in online trading, individual investors can now—for the first time ever—retain complete control over their orders. From funneling an order directly to an electronic communication network (ECN) to routing an order to a specific market maker's desk through Nasdaq's SelectNet system, almost nothing is out of bounds for today's direct access trader.

But you don't have to take my word it. For proof of the strength of direct access traders, just take a peek at some recent statistics. The Bear Stearns study found that "semiprofessionals" trading with their own capital make an average of 875,000 trades per day[1]—or roughly 47 percent of all daily Internet stock trades—even though they comprise less than 1 percent of the total of 12.5 million U.S. online stock trading accounts.[2] Put simply, the direct access trader has changed the American stock market landscape dramatically.

In this book we will cover all the techniques this new breed of trader employs to maximize profits and minimize losses. From learning the ins and outs of such key strategies as "scalping" and swing trading to managing risk and adhering to the golden rules of day trading, we will provide a roadmap of the preferred tactics and tools of the successful direct access trader. What's more, through in-depth case studies, we will provide a rare behind-the-scenes look at the intraday mind-set of different types of traders.

Many of the early chapters of this book will be devoted to the dos and don'ts of direct access online trading. For example, for each and every trade you make, it is important to set up a systematic trading plan that includes—at a minimum—an entry point, a stop loss, and an exit target. On the other hand, it is illogical and risky to hold onto losing stocks overnight, and it is a mistake to get too emotional over a big winner or a string of losses.

We also will examine the distinguishing features of the Nasdaq level II public quote screen, explore the pros and cons of specific order-routing mechanisms and execution destinations, and provide examples of how to build your electronic trading portfolio using different strategies.

In later chapters of the book we will discuss the ebb and flow of the market in relation to risk management. Along the way, we will talk about the importance of maintaining discipline and check out the reasons many short-term day traders also hold long-term positions. Moreover, we will outline when to use different types of stop orders, analyze the merits of back-testing trading strategies, and discuss the steps you need to take to protect yourself while trading on margin.

After the risk-management section, we will take a look at the different levels of volatility tied to specific stocks and industry sectors and pinpoint the types of stocks that best fit specific trading strategies.

Lastly, the book will take you deep inside the direct access thought process, providing a screen-by-screen breakdown and analysis of positions different traders take during the course of a typical trading day.

This said, prior to reading about all these tactics and techniques, it is important to have an understanding of the evolution of the direct access trader. Therefore, in the rest of this chapter we will examine the regulatory changes and technological advancements that vaulted individual investors into the position that they hold today. Specifically, we are going to provide details on the Securities and Exchange Commission's order handling rules, the rise of ECNs, and the subsequent emergence of the direct access broker.

THE ORDER HANDLING RULES AND THE EVOLUTION OF ECNs

By the time the second half of the 1990s rolled around, the U.S. stock markets had already undergone a period of transformation. Online discount brokers had sprung up all over the place, unbundling advice from trading commissions. Moreover, these new entities offered much cheaper commissions than traditional phone-based brokers, leading many average Americans to rediscover the art of stock trading.

As more and more of these online discounters popped up, trying to undercut each other on commissions, more investors began dabbling in short-term trades. Prior to the start of 1997, however, individual investors trading stocks in America were still plagued by significant disadvantages—especially in the Nasdaq market. The quotes being displayed in the public domain were not all-inclusive, and the execution destination choices were limited, making it nearly impossible for nonprofessional traders to compete head-on with market makers for the best prices.

Market makers, in fact, could place superior quotes on private alternative trading networks without informing the rest of the investing public. Moreover, they had the ability to mask retail limit orders—orders in which individual investors specify an exact price at which they want to buy or sell a stock.

Eventually, these practices led to allegations that a number of market makers were lining their own pockets by artificially widening the spread—the difference between the best bid and the best offer for a stock. These charges were quite serious in nature because market makers maintain a two-sided quote for every stock they trade, profiting from the spread.

In January 1997, however, in an effort to wipe out price collusion and level the stock playing field for the individual investor, the Securities and Exchange Commission (SEC) stepped in and implemented the order handling rules. The new regulations, which included the limit order display rule and the quote display rule, required market makers to publicly display best bids and offers for all orders of 10,000 shares or less—regardless of whether they are trading those orders in private or public markets. Perhaps more significantly, the rules opened the floodgates to a new species of market maker competitor known as ECNs—equity trade-matching systems that would one day become the great equalizer for individual investors.

The limit order display rule forever changed the way market makers handled price-specific orders. Before 1997, a market maker who received a limit order that was priced better than his or her own inside quote for a stock was not required to publicly display that quote. If they so chose, market makers could execute these orders anonymously or reroute them to a fellow market maker. In this scenario, since the limit order was not being displayed in the public domain, individual investors were not aware that there was actually a better price out there.

However, the display rule stipulated that within 30 seconds of receiving a superior-priced limit order, a market maker must either (1) incorporate the limit order into his or her own public quote, (2) execute the order, or (3) electronically route the order to an ECN. The latter two options would prove to be particularly appealing for market makers who did not want to advertise the prices and sizes of limit orders they were holding.

The rule effectively eliminated the ability of market makers to hide superior retail limit orders. Consequently, individual investors profited from better order representation, and ECNs became the favorite dumping ground for unwanted limit orders from market makers. What's more, because the rule empowered individual investors to quote inside the current best bid and ask, it also helped to narrow spreads significantly. Put simply, if a market maker holds the best price for a given stock at 42 and receives a limit order for 42⅛, then—in accordance with the display rule—that order becomes the inside market for that stock.

Meanwhile, the SEC's second order handling rule prohibited market makers from placing superior quotes on private alternative trading networks without reflecting the same price in the Nasdaq montage—the public quote screen that is accessible to all Nasdaq participants.

In the pre-order handling era, market makers at times would list one quote on the Nasdaq montage and simultaneously maintain a different quote for the same stock on Reuters' Instinet Corp.—the agency brokerage giant that operated the only ECN in town. Unencumbered by regulatory prohibitions, Instinet's ECN enabled both market makers and large institutional investors to secretly snag the best stock prices—often at the expense of Mr. Joe Average investor.

However, the so-called quote rule, which actually was an amendment to an earlier rule instituted by the SEC, ended this practice of secretive trades executed among high-powered friends. Market makers were restricted from placing superior quotes on Instinet, or any other private trading network, without reflecting that price in the Nasdaq montage.

Collectively, the rules brought quotes that had been either masked by market makers or hidden on private networks into the public domain. Individual investors reaped rewards from narrower spreads, improved price transparency and better order representation, and the SEC achieved many of its preconceived small investor–targeted fairness goals.

Just as significantly, the rules supplied ECNs with the ammunition they needed to grow and flourish. Beyond providing ECNs with a mechanism for capturing significant retail order flow, the rules also brought the new equity trade-matching systems into the public consciousness. ECNs, in conjunction with the rules, were required to post their best bids and offers for all orders between 100 and 10,000 shares on Nasdaq's public quote screen.

This public quote dissemination mandate gave young, upstart ECNs— such as Datek Holdings' Island—the exposure they required to build much-needed liquidity. Although Instinet would remain the ECN Goliath, it would no longer operate an equity trade-matching system monopoly in Nasdaq stocks. And the ECN marketplace, fueled by public exposure and retail limit order flow, would expand quite rapidly.

Today, there are nine ECNs: Instinet, Island, REDIBook, Archipelago, Brut, Bloomberg Tradebook, NexTrade, MarketXT, and Attain.[3] Unlike market makers, these networks are not required to maintain both sides of a quote in a trade and do not profit from the spread. Rather, each of the ECNs functions as an electronic limit order book, making profits by charging small fees for every buyer and seller it matches up.

The emergence of these networks in many ways spurred a tremendous boom in the electronic day trading industry. For the full-time day trader, ECNs provide many advantages. First and foremost, ECNs give such individuals an anonymous electronic forum to trade directly with each other, without any assistance from traditional broker/dealer intermediaries. Second, ECNs allow clients to trade in increments thinner than sixteenths—quotes smaller than market makers deal in. This is significant because in the predecimalization world, the ability to trade in smaller price increments often led to individuals finding superior quotes on ECNs. And better prices ultimately translate into cheaper execution costs.

Moreover, if these reasons are not enough to entice an individual to route an order to an ECN, he or she may be lured by the fact that ECNs typically supply faster executions than market makers. In the future, through sophisticated technology that we will examine later in this chapter, individuals may be able to electronically route an order directly to the trading desks of specific market makers. Today, however, individual investors who want to send an order to a specific market maker have to route that order through Nasdaq's SelectNet—an order-routing system that is not exactly renowned for its speed.

ECNs, on the other hand, allow individuals to tap into their order books directly. This direct connectivity translates into superior speed, because the quicker an order gets to your desired execution destination, the more likely you are to get a fill either at or near your desired price. In fact, ECNs often provide fills in less than 1 second.

These factors combined have propelled ECNs to great success—not just among the day trader segment but in the overall Nasdaq market as well. Currently, the nine ECNs account for roughly one-third of Nasdaq's total volume.[4] What's more, according to a May 2000 study performed by Celent Communications, ECNs are going to be responsible for more than 50 percent of Nasdaq's total volume by 2003.[5]

While some ECNs, such as Island and Attain, cater specifically to day traders, others, such as Instinet's market-leading network, are targeted primarily at large buy-side institutions. This customer diversity is one factor driving the ECNs' winning formula. The telltale sign of the success and influence of ECNs, however, is found in their prestigious list of owners.

In an effort to hedge their bets on the future of the U.S. stock market structure, almost every major Wall Street broker/dealer—including Goldman Sachs, Morgan Stanley Dean Witter, and Credit Suisse First Boston—have taken minority stakes in multiple ECNs.[6] Moreover, a few of the largest online brokers—such as Datek (Island), E*TRADE (Archipelago), and Charles Schwab (REDIBook)—have invested in ECNs.

Not to be left out, a couple of day trading firms also have entered into the ECN ownership arena. Attain, for example, is owned by All-Tech Direct, a Montvale, N.J.–based day trading firm. And MarketXT, the newest ECN entrant, recently was acquired by Tradescape.com, a direct access broker that also happens to own the large day trading firm Momentum Securities.

However, for all the good that ECNs have done for electronic day traders, the relationship between the two parties is certainly a reciprocal one. Full-time day traders operating out of professional day trading shops such as Momentum provide lots of order flow to ECNs, making them more viable. Moreover, people who make their living trading stocks from their home PCs are also boosting the liquidity of ECNs.

DIRECT ACCESS VERSUS TRADITIONAL ONLINE BROKERS

The order handling rules, as we now know, spawned the rise of ECNs. But the success of ECNs had wild, market-changing ramifications of its own. Once the public got wind of the advantages of ECNs, the demand for direct connectivity to those networks grew significantly. Hence, in the late 1990s, we saw the advent of the so-called direct access broker. Through advanced portal software, these brokers could provide nearly instantaneous direct access to multiple ECNs.

This enhanced access, in turn, led to the birth of a new, extremely powerful breed of investors known as direct access traders. However, the simple chronology of events does not paint a complete picture of the giant step forward direct access trading represents.

By allowing individual investors to connect electronically straight into a specific equity trade-matching system, direct access brokers have empowered individuals with unprecedented autonomy over their orders. Direct access traders, using the ECN portal software, can now be certain that their orders are being sent to the appropriate execution destination.

Moreover, they can be reasonably sure that if there is an order out there that matches up with their own, it is going to get filled very quickly.

This method of order control is a very recent phenomenon, however. In fact, prior to the ECN-induced launch of direct access brokers, highly active online traders depended primarily on traditional online brokerage systems to route orders and receive fills. And unfortunately, most of the traditional discounters do not offer direct connectivity.

Instead, many of these brokers reroute orders they receive from individuals directly to wholesale market makers in a controversial practice known as *payment for order flow*.[7] Under this arrangement, the online broker, after receiving an individual investor's buy or sell order, electronically routes the potential trade to a market maker in return for a small payment—or "rebate"—that typically is one penny per share. Simultaneously, the market maker also pays for other orders, matching them together and profiting from the spread.

In simple terms, online brokers who exchange orders for payment are neither scanning the market to find the best price nor providing investors with the opportunity to do so. The end result: Individuals, who are sometimes unaware that their orders are being sold off, often receive inferior prices and slower executions.

Ken Johnson, chief executive officer of the sixthmarket.com—an Austin, Texas–based firm that teaches courses in online trading—says that active online traders who still route orders through nondirect brokers such as Ameritrade and E*TRADE are taking on unacceptable risks. "What you're not able to see [via those platforms] is where your order is getting executed," he says. "You're not getting good fills. You don't understand how to get the best price in the market. And if the market is really moving away from you in a time of stress, you're going to get slaughtered."

Direct access brokers, in stark contrast to their online discount predecessors, provide traders with the ability to electronically route orders directly to the matching engines of ECNs. "Rather than just clicking on the button that says 'buy' and having no control over where an order is sent, . . . [a trader] now has complete control over the execution. If you want to send it to a specific ECN or preference a specific market maker, you can," says Greg Smith, the lead analyst covering the electronic brokerage sector at San Francisco–based research and consulting firm Hambrecht & Quist.

Somewhat surprisingly, a large number of traders still use traditional online brokers. In terms of average daily trades and volume, however, the direct access, or "semiprofessional," traders dominate active traders and self-directed asset managers—the other two types of online investors identified in the Bear Stearns report. The study found that the longer-term-oriented "asset managers" represented nearly 69 percent of all online accounts but only 3 percent of daily online trades. The "active traders," on the other hand, represented roughly 31 percent of online accounts and 20 percent of online trades. However, the latter figure clearly pales in comparison with the total number of daily trades performed by direct access traders.

Including both nonproprietary traders (who trade on behalf of their own accounts) and proprietary traders (who risk capital on behalf of their firms), traders using direct access systems are responsible for a whopping 76.4 percent of all daily online trades, according to the study. In addition, direct access traders—who typically make between 25 and 40 trades per day—are significantly more profitable than either self-directed asset managers or active traders—who average 25 to 50 trades per year.

The study found that direct access traders are 165 times more profitable than the former group and "exponentially more profitable" than the latter group. Specifically, in terms of pretax earnings, the study estimated that direct access traders generate 2677 basis points per asset under control, whereas self-directed asset managers and active traders generate 16 and 53 basis points, respectively.[8]

Sixthmarket.com's Johnson says the reason direct access traders hold such a large edge over other online investors is that the technology they use gives them great freedom and flexibility. "With direct access, you're looking at the market and you happen to see that REDIBook happens to have the best bid on a stock, and that's who you want to hit. So you just hit that [quote directly] and get the best price available at that second," he explains.

What's more, Johnson says that as individual investors gain more knowledge, direct access systems will make significant penetration into the "active trader" market. "I think that as the public becomes aware . . . they're going to be very upset over what has happened to them unknowingly in these payment for order flow systems," he says.

Hambrecht and Quest's Smith, while asserting that payment for order flow arrangements will continue to exist in "one form or another," concurs that the public will eventually become less tolerant of this practice. "Anything that induces someone to send their order flow directly to them is a form of payment for order flow," he says. "It will always be around, but there will be much more disclosure about it. And people will know about it and understand it much more than they do today."

Greater understanding of payment for order flow undoubtedly will lead to a larger and wider audience of clients for direct access brokers—a group that Smith describes as the "fastest growing" segment of the brokerage community. In time, he says, direct access systems will appeal not only to professional day traders but also to any type of "sophisticated investor."

A Bear Stearns spokesperson, meanwhile, says that as software provided by the likes of CyBerCorp, Tradescape.com, and Tradecast Securities becomes "more commonplace" and cheaper to access, more and more investors in the active trader community will migrate from online discount brokers to direct access brokers.[9] Traders, he says, will realize that direct access systems enable them to retain tighter control of their profits and losses.

"With direct access, you're seeing all the prices that are out there, . . . and you can execute that trade immediately," the spokesperson says. "Those traders . . . have a lot more control over the actual trade, and where it's executed and how it's executed, than they would by [routing it through] E*TRADE or Ameritrade."

ORDER-ROUTING OPTIONS

In some cases, direct access brokers are providing direct links not only to all nine ECNs but also to Nasdaq's SelectNet and Small Order Execution System (SOES) order-routing applications. Through SOES, direct access traders can send their buy and sell orders to the desks of market makers—the large contingent of broker/dealers that controls the price range for Nasdaq stocks. Market makers are required to fill all open SOES market orders, which are orders to buy or sell a stock at the market's best available price.

However, the maximum order size for SOES is 1000 shares, and market makers are required to fill only the number of shares they have previously stated they are willing to buy or sell for a specific stock. For instance, if you place an order to buy 500 shares of stock XYZ but the market maker is displaying 300 shares available on SOES, then the market maker is only obligated to fill 300 shares—if the prices match up.

SelectNet, like SOES, is a mechanism that direct access traders can use to route orders to market makers. In contrast to SOES, however,

SelectNet has no order size restrictions and—on top of funneling orders to market makers—can link to ECNs. More significantly, investors have to wait at least 10 seconds to cancel SelectNet orders—a sliver of time that can seem like an eternity for highly volatile Nasdaq stocks.

Dissimilar to SOES, SelectNet also comprises two types of orders: broadcast and preference. A SelectNet broadcast order is visible, exclusively, to the full complement of Nasdaq market makers. A SelectNet preference order, on the other hand, will route only to a specific market maker or ECN "preferenced" by the trader.

Generally speaking, while SOES and SelectNet do offer a few advantages, direct access traders usually can find superior quotes and experience faster executions through direct connections to ECNs. Moreover, orders posted on both SOES and SelectNet are not displayed on Nasdaq level II—Nasdaq's dynamically updating public quote montage.

On the other hand, when an individual routes an order directly to an ECN, that order is represented on the Nasdaq level II screen—as long as it is a specific ECN's best bid or offer for that particular stock. Level II, of course, is a quote screen that displays the best bids and offers for a specific stock from every market maker and ECN that is showing interest in that stock. Nasdaq level I—Nasdaq's other public quote screen—reflects only the very best bid and offer for a given stock.

This said, while direct connectivity to ECNs now presents benefits in terms of price, speed, and order representation, technological advancements may entice direct access traders to send orders to market makers more often in the future. At lease one direct access broker (Tradescape) has developed technology that enables individuals to send orders directly to the desks of specific market makers. Of course, this eliminates the tedious—and often costly—step of routing an order to a market maker via either SelectNet or SOES.

Tradescape, for its part, has built an internal network that electronically connects its Smart Order Routing Technology (SORT) engine directly to the desks of a group of market makers. And while no other direct access brokers have, to date, developed direct connectivity to market makers, just about every one of Tradescape's rivals has built some type of intelligent order-routing algorithm. These algorithms, which factor in a trader's desired price and size, automatically hunt and seek multiple ECNs and market makers to find the best quote for a specific stock.

Among the most popular of these intelligent order-routing mechanisms are CyBerCorp's CyberXchange and Tradescape's SORT.

CyberXchange tracks all the best bids and offers for a stock through electronic interfaces it has to all nine ECNs and more than 50 market makers. After identifying the counterparty who is offering the best price at the specific volume level a trader requested, the system then forwards an order—directly and electronically—to that counterparty. Similarly, Tradescape's newest version of SORT consolidates many sources of liquidity in an effort to hunt down the best price but also measures latency time—or the time it takes for SORT to contact an execution destination and receive an acknowledgment back.

Not surprisingly, emphasizing that they already have direct connectivity to Wall Street's most liquid execution destinations, some traders scoff at the notion of entrusting the search for the best price for a given security to a machine. However, Hambrecht and Quist's Smith thinks that intelligent order-routing mechanisms have excellent growth potential—particularly in the active trader community. "It's pretty sophisticated stuff that I think will really migrate up to the mainstream in the years ahead," he says.

These intelligent order-routing systems are not a smart tool for professional day traders who exclusively trade limit orders, says Peter Sweeney, a direct access trader who engages primarily in swing trades. However, he says that these systems are used "quite often" by full-time traders who are entering market orders. The traders entering market orders, Sweeney notes, are more interested in getting complete fills at a reasonable price than in receiving the very best quotes. And efficient, intelligent order-routing systems will find prices at least near the inside market.

Speaking on the condition of anonymity, a different direct access trader says that using an intelligent order-routing system really only makes sense for traders who attack the market by trading a plethora of stocks. This type of trader, says the source, has the very difficult—and sometimes overwhelming—task of finding the best prices for a large group of stocks. Nevertheless, traders who use the intelligent order-routing component of their direct access system can simplify their quote quests.

For many reasons, direct access technology is beginning to hit its stride in the Nasdaq market. And as the popularity of direct access systems continues to grow, so too will the number of platforms individual investors can choose from. Smith says that traditional online brokers—cognizant of the fact that a small continent of influential clients of direct access brokers—are exploring ways in which to provide better services to their customers.

Some traditional discounters, he says, may follow in the footsteps of Charles Schwab Corp., which filled its direct access void by acquiring CyBerCorp in February 2000. Other brokers, Smith says, likely will meet the demands of sophisticated investors by licensing direct access software. Either way, says Smith, all the "big online brokers" will have a direct access solution by the first quarter of 2001.

NOTES

1. Amy S. Butte, Bear Stearns, Financial Technology, Day Trading and Beyond, www.bearstearns.com, Exhibit 8, p. 9.

2. Bear Stearns, Exhibit 1, p. 6.

3. Sang Lee, Octavio Marenzi, and Jody Cornish, Profiling the ECNs, Celent Communications, www.celent.com, Table 4, p. 40.

4. Celent Communications, Figure 1, p. 6.

5. Celent Communications, Figure 2, p. 7.

6. Celent Communications, Table 3, p. 39.

7. Bear Stearns, Exhibit 4, p. 7.

8. Bear Stearns, Exhibit 8, p. 9.

9. Bear Stearns, Exhibit 9, p. 11.

2

THE RULES

To consistently rake in profits as a direct access trader, you must equip yourself with a roadmap for success. Going into each trading day, you should have a game plan that outlines which stocks you want to trade, how much you want to gain, and how much you are willing to risk. On top of this, you should have an idea as to the length of time you are willing to hold specific stocks and the number of shares you would like to trade.

But just how should you go about figuring all this out? Well, one sure-fire way to prepare yourself for each trading day is to obey the rules of direct access trading. Although there is no official list of standard methods for making money, most traders agree that you will make positive strides if you adhere to the following quintet of rules:

1   *Trade against a plan.* Prior to every trade, identify your entry point, stop loss, and exit target—the three basic elements of a systematic plan.

2   *Follow your stop loss.* If you tell yourself you are going to cut your losses after a stock has dropped to a certain price, stick to that guideline.

3   *Do not take home losing positions.* Holding onto any position overnight used to be taboo for direct access traders. But now the overwhelming majority of traders agree that it is okay to hold on to stocks overnight—as long as they are winning positions with momentum on their side.

4   *Get out at your exit target on winning trades.* It is easy to get caught up in the emotion of a winner, and if you do not adhere to your predefined exit, the profit you made could easily turn into a loss.

5   *Never trade what you cannot afford to lose.* Since this requires you to check your ego at the door, it is easier said than done. Successful traders, however, are keenly aware of their capitalization level and are able to maintain discipline.

THE PLAN PAYOFF

Whether you are a scalper or a swing trader, whether you trade 100 times a day or 10 times a day, whether your risk-reward ratio is 5:1 or 2:1, these rules—when followed closely—will provide the discipline you need to take a greater percentage of winning positions. Moreover, they will supply you with a mechanism for avoiding big mistakes and protecting against large losses.

Although all the rules are important, rule 1 is perhaps the most significant—especially for less experienced direct access traders. "One of the biggest mistakes that traders make is that they really don't have any type of methodology to what they're doing. They get into a trade, sometimes just on the spur of the moment, and once they're in, they're not sure how much they're willing to risk," says Ralph Cruz, co-chief executive officer of Omega Research—a research and software firm that provides market analysis tools for traders.

Prior to each trade, Cruz says, you have to have an "idea" about why you are taking a position, the amount you are willing to risk, and what your profit expectations are. Moreover, you should know the types of stocks you want to trade before the trading day starts.

The different elements of a systematic plan, Cruz says, allow a trader to tackle all of these issues. Just as significantly, when carefully conceived and strictly followed, a plan makes it possible for a trader to separate his or her emotions from his or her decision-making process. "You must trade with a plan for each and every trade, without exception," emphasizes sixthmarket.com's CEO Ken Johnson. "If you don't know this, you've got no business trading."

Of course, pinpointing your entry price represents the starting line for any systematic plan. Before you do anything else, you must figure out the price at which you would like to buy or sell a specific stock. But how, exactly, do you go about doing this? Well, one option is to create a set of criteria that triggers a buy or sell order.

An order could be triggered, for example, when a stock breaks through a key resistance level while simultaneously recording strong volume. These criteria, obviously, should set a trade into motion. And by demanding that certain criteria must be met, traders can weed out the good trades from the bad ones. "Anyone who has traded actively knows there is a lot of false noise in the market. There are a lot of false indications, such as false breakouts. . . . So you really need to look for multiple things [before you enter a trade]," Cruz says.

This said, while you may be looking to enter into a stock at, say, 42⅛, this does not necessarily mean that you cannot adjust this price— by an eight or a quarter up or down. When buying long, such an adjustment is known as your *chase point*.

"Ever since the introduction of the order handling rules, there has not been enough liquidity in the SOES system to ever count on getting everything at your entry price. If a trade is good [for you] at 42⅛, then there is a good chance it's [also] going to be good for you at 42¼," says Johnson.

Smart traders, he says, will factor their chase point—or "slippage amount"—into their entry position. Having a chase point, adds Johnson, will give you a better chance of getting the trade you really wanted. In fact, Johnson suggests that a direct access trader should place a limit order that is "slightly above" his or her ideal entry price. In this way, even if you do not get the exact price you want, you may end up with a fill that at least comes close to meeting your risk-reward expectations.

Speaking of risk-reward, the amount you are willing to chase a stock should be directly proportional to your risk-reward ratio (which measures the amount you are willing to lose versus the amount you want to gain).

At least, this is the opinion of Howard Abell, a trading guru who is the cofounder of invest2know.com—a financial education site targeted at on-line traders.

Abell, who has traded equities, futures, and options contracts in the United States for the past 30 years, describes himself as a "pattern trader" who typically looks to gain 2 or 3 points while risking 1 point. Given these risk-reward parameters, he says that he sometimes has "room" to adjust his entry price. "Some people overdo the entry point. For example, they might put in a limit order for a stock at 43. And the market goes to 43⅛, and so they can't buy it at 43," Abell explains. "But my tendency there is to just go to the market and pay the ⅛. In the kind of trading that I do and recommend for other people to do, ⅛ of a point shouldn't matter."

Like Johnson and Abell, Sweeney—a full-time active online trader who works in a day trading office in Connecticut—believes that there are times when a trader should leave a small price window open when entering a trade. Specifically, Sweeney says that he leaves room to chase a stock when he "buys strength and sells weakness."

After figuring out your entry price and chase point (if any), the next thing you must do—if you are trading against a plan—is identify your stop loss. In addition to protecting against large losses, knowing your stop loss can play a key role in your selection of stocks to trade.

Before the start of each trading day, Johnson says, it is wise to make up a list of potentially good stocks. In part, he says, you can determine whether a stock is right for you by looking at intraday and historical chart patterns. However, just because a stock looks good on a chart, it may not be the right one for you—particularly if the price range of the stock does not jive with your stop loss.

For example, says Johnson, some traders never set their stop loss more than $2 away from their entry point. Therefore, keeping the amount they are willing to lose in mind, these traders can effectively eliminate extremely volatile stocks from their list of potential setups. "You already know that you can't get into those stocks and adhere to your stop loss. So you cross those off your list," he says.

The price range of a stock also comes into play when you are iden-tifying the final component of a systematic plan—the exit target. Abell says that active online traders research the stocks they like to trade and have a "strong sense" of what the price range—or "wiggle factor"—is for those securities. Many traders, in fact, identify their exit target based on the average price fluctuations of a stock.

"Say, for example, wiggle factor is 1 full point for a $50 stock. If it goes to 52, then [a trader] would probably be wise to get out," says Abell "It's part of the preparation people do to maximize their returns, . . . [and] you can determine that stock by stock."

All in all, having a plan in place before you "pull the trigger" should have a positive impact on your trades. Recently, however, Johnson says he taught a course where only 1 of 30 direct access trading students said that he could identify his entry point, stop loss, and exit target for the stocks he planned to trade. "The other 29 people [were] at risk," according to Johnson.

Generally speaking, following all the elements of a systematic plan generates good results for direct access traders. However, Sweeney, for his part, believes that your plan does not have to be carved in stone. "You can't go in and say, 'Let me buy this,' and not have an idea where it's going or how much you're willing to risk. . . . [But] things can change, and you have to be willing to adjust to the market," notes Sweeney.

Evolving market conditions may force you to tweak your plan during the course of a day. For example, Sweeney says, if you trade a stock that typically has volume of 300,000 shares a day, but all of the sudden you see a number of block trades to buy 50,000 shares of the stock, you will know that a market maker has a large buyer for that stock, and you adjust your plan accordingly.

STAYING TRUE TO YOUR STOP

No matter what type of direct access trader you are, waving the white flag of surrender when you are holding a losing position can be a very difficult task. Mentally, you may just not be ready to give in, hoping beyond hope that a tumbling stock is going to shoot back up in the market at any moment. In order to minimize your losses, however, you have to dump stocks before they fall beneath the price level you set as your maximum risk.

In trading circles, this practice is known as *staying true to your stop loss.* Later on in this book we will be taking a look at the different types of stops traders use, including those which keep you in the black. Right now, however, we are going to examine the traditional stop loss, in which traders exit a trade somewhere below their entry point.

Not allowing a stock to sink below a set stop loss is one rule that many traders adhere to. For example, if you buy a stock at 52¾ and set a stop loss at 51⅛, you should not let the stock slip past 51⅛. "What hurts most people, and makes them unsuccessful, is their inability to take the loss, given any parameter that they decide," says Abell. "The essential ingredient is that you must think of active online trading as a process, and not as a series of individual trades. That way, if your methodology is sound, whether you make 100 trades or 1000 trades, you will be successful in a certain percentage of those. You'll reap a larger reward than your risk profile, and therefore, you'll be a net positive."

Abell says that traders who claim they have no loss objectives are "fooling themselves," because minimizing risk is a key for any successful trader. And the secret of minimizing risk, he says, is to absorb your losses when your stock hits your stop level.

The important thing to remember is that no single trade is overly important. Keeping this philosophy in mind, after you have made a trade, you must "move on to the next trade," no matter whether you have locked in a profit or absorbed a substantial loss, says Abell.

Unfortunately, sticking to your stop loss is much easier said than done—particularly when a trader runs into a series of losses. However, while he concedes that staying true to your stop loss is not an easy concept to follow, Abell says that you have to remember that "profitable trades will more than offset your losses if you're disciplined enough and your methodology is robust."

Omega's Cruz, meanwhile, says that some traders have a tragic tendency to not be willing to admit when they make mistakes. They create a plan that specifies that they are going to hold a stock only for a preset period of time, but when a loss sets in, the stop-loss component of the plan is thrown out the window. "Then, all of a sudden, you're down three times the amount you wanted to risk, simply because you can't pull the trigger and get out of the trade and admit that you were wrong," explains Cruz.

One of the mistakes that traders sometimes make is not only holding onto a losing stock but also buying more of it as it tumbles downward. This practice is known *averaging down*. "There is nobody in this business that hasn't done it [at least once] . . . You're thinking I'm smarter than the market. You just don't want to take the loss. You feel weak and vulnerable, and you can't steer up the courage to take the loss and walk away," says Sweeney.

From personal experience, Sweeney says he can recall at least one trader whose objective was to make 10 points in a single trade but who actually wound up losing 6 or 7 points. "I had the mental stop loss in place but didn't adhere to it. Not only that, but I actually bought more of the losing stock," the trader said.

A different direct access trader, speaking on condition of anonymity, says that determining where to set a stop loss is contingent on the amount of time a trader plans to hold a specific stock. Before entering a stop loss, he says, a trader must estimate the price swing that's going to take place in that stock during the time he's holding it. "I will incorporate a stop loss into every order. While it does vary, it's really important to have that to prevent really down days," says the trader.

In the final analysis, Abell says, if you have a successful trading methodology, you have to stick with it—even if this means that you have to bear the brunt of a string of losses. Your stop loss will help limit the damage you incur, and Abell says that there is therefore no need to change the parameters under which you are working—as long as you have had success in the past.

Most important, he says, you cannot be afraid to jump on the next opportunity after a series of bad trades. Abell—who believes that a direct access trader should never risk more than 1 percent of his or her equity— says that you have to remember that the next trade you make could be the one that "wipes out" all your previous losses.

THE OVERNIGHT OPTION

In the past, active online traders simply stayed away from holding positions overnight. Too much could happen—rumors could spread or bad news could break—in between the close of the market and the opening the next day. While some traders still consider it taboo to stick with a stock for 2 days or more, most now believe that it is all right to hold overnight positions.

There is, however, one caveat: You should stay with a stock after the close only if it is a winner with momentum on its side. "I don't know of a day trader that believes you shouldn't hold positions overnight anymore. Also, I don't know of a day trader who thinks that you should hold on to a loser overnight," says Johnson.

In the long run, it serves most people well to get out of a losing stock before the end of the day, concurs Abell. By following this rule, he says, you force yourself to stay with stocks that have positive momentum. However, Abell also says that more experienced traders—like himself—have developed "something of an instinct to read the way a market is acting and therefore do not necessarily need to dump a stock just because it has lost a little ground and the end of the day is nearing."

"You need to look at more of the swing trade nature of the stock market. If the stock hasn't violated your parameters [during the course of a day], there may not be any reason for you to get out—even though it doesn't show a profit. If you buy something at 50 and it closes at 49¾, but it never violated any of your parameters, and the market was quiet and didn't do anything, does that really mean you should just get out? I'm not sure about that."

Still, no matter how experienced you are, sticking with trades overnight is definitely not beneficial for every type of trader. For example, if you are a scalper—or a trader who is looking to profit from extremely small price fluctuations in a stock over short periods of time—then holding on to positions after the close of the market does not make sense for you. "If you're a scalper, you have no business taking positions home overnight," Sweeney says.

GETTING OUT WHILE THE GETTING IS GOOD

When it comes to maximizing your profit, one of the most important rules to obey is getting out at your exit target on winning trades. If a stock has met your expectations in terms of profit, the wise thing to do is to cash in before the trade turns around on you. "Once you determine your exit point in any position, never waver," says Abell, emphasizing that he does not use the word *never* lightly.

Of course, following this advice is not as easy as it sounds. It is very tempting for people to stay with a winning trade after it has gapped up to their exit target. In part, this unwillingness to let go of a trade is brought on by greed. But such an attitude also has something to do with the fact that the act of quickly buying or selling a stock is unnatural and takes time for people to get comfortable with.

This is why, Abell says, he instructs inexperienced traders to perform between 100 and 200 "scratch trades"—or trades where you buy or sell a stock at the exact same price—prior to actively participating in the direct access arena. "Psychologically, you say, 'I just bought [the stock], how can I sell it 5 minutes later?' " explains Abell. "That is the most inhibiting idea that people face when doing active trading. . . . [But] once you get beyond that point, you're well on your way to success."

The importance of getting out at your exit target cannot be understated, because a profitable trade potentially can turn into a big loser in the blink of an eye, says sixthmarket.com's Johnson. Too often, he says, traders do not lock in their profits. "They have a target for their profit, and they don't take it," says Johnson. "Say my exit target is up around 50. It gets up to 50 or 51, and I think, 'Man, I'll ride this to 60.' The next thing you know, it's at 35, and I've lost money on it."

Mentally, it can be extra tough for you to recover and do the right thing if you had a chance to lock in profits on a trade but passed it up only to eventually find yourself in the red. If you had a chance to make $5000, for example, you may think that you cannot afford to take a loss now—because you have lost $5000 on top of the money you invested initially. And then, all of a sudden, as the stock continues to tumble, you may realize that you have done something extremely irresponsible—like put your kid's college fund at risk, says Johnson. "A lot of the time, the market doesn't give you a second chance," he says. "I've seen people completely wipe themselves out—all because they knew where to get out but just wouldn't do it."

Undoubtedly, you also can lose your shirt if you go against rule 5: Never trade more than you can afford to lose. Inevitably, however, losing traders, at some point in their careers, break this rule. And that one bad trade, if it does not bust you, leads to others. "Once you put stress on your pocketbook and your emotions, you make very bad decisions. And so you're going to continue to make bad decisions if you're that stressed," theorizes Abell.

GUIDING LIGHT

Above and beyond the rules we have just discussed, there is a larger group of guidelines that point the way to success for many direct access traders. These are somewhat more flexible than the aforementioned rules, and the importance of each guideline depends on the level of experience and specific style of individual traders.

Generally speaking, however, guidelines provide traders with sound tidbits of advice. These pieces of advice include the following:

* *Know thyself.* No, we are not trying to take you back to the days when you studied Greek philosophers. The message here is that it

is important to know what your motivation is for trading. All trading success starts with self-awareness. You have to know what your motivation is for trading, and it cannot begin and end with a desire to make money, says Johnson. "Anyone who tells me they want to trade to make a bunch of money, I already know that they're going to fail. The reason I know you're going to fail is because you are going to go out and try to trade, and I will promise you are [at least initially] going to lose some money," says Johnson. "You're going to then conclude that trading is not for you, and you're going to quit. And you're going to quit a loser, and you're going to have lost money, because your only goal was to make money." Johnson claims he has seen this exact scenario unfold for "thousands" of traders. To avoid falling into this trap, he says, investors should at first set out to "master the challenge" of direct access trading. Adopting such a mantra, says Johnson, will give a trader the strength to "cut through big losses."

- *Do not put all your eggs in one basket.* If you spread out your trading capital among a diverse portfolio of stocks, you potentially can reduce your risk because no single trade is going to kill you. However, that is not to say that you cannot be successful trading only one or two stocks—as long as you possess expert knowledge of those issues and watch them like a hawk. Abell says that the reason some traders shun diversification is because they do not have the "equity" needed to trade a large group of stocks on a short-term basis. The problem with tracking and trading only one or two stocks, however, is that traders tend to get attached to them and are reluctant to take losses. "They get emotionally invested in these one or two positions, and they feel that if they get out, they won't have a better opportunity. But truth is they're losing opportunity if they continue to stay with a losing stock," says Abell.

- *Research the market makers who trade the stocks you are interested in.* To get a feel for the market for a stock, you must be knowledgeable about the market makers who actually trade that issue. By becoming familiar with the market makers, you also will begin to understand the trends for a stock—whether it is over the course of a day or even an hour. "A lot of people will just look at a given stock, and say 'Oh, this looks good. There's a lot volume on it. I think I can scalp for a ¹⁄₁₆ or ⅛ here and there,' and just start trading it. But before you do that, you should spend weeks, if possible, to really research the market makers [who make markets] in the stocks you want to trade," says one anonymous trader. If you do not know the market for a stock that you are in, this source says, you could get burned. A short while ago, this trader says, he was actively trading a hot net infrastructure stock that he knew very little about. Unfortunately, the source says, his ignorance caused him to take a significant loss in that stock. "I thought I saw a trend for the stock, but I really hadn't researched it at all," the source says.

- *Do not trade against a trend.* This guideline is really very simple: If the overall market is weak, it is not a wise time to go on a buying spree—and vice versa. Some traders try to fight a weak market by buying a stock when it hits rock bottom. However, Abell says the smart money in a market spiraling downward lies with traders who sell rallies. "One mistake that most people make is that in a weak market, they're looking to pick the bottom, because they think that's where the most opportunity lies. But in fact, in a weak market, the opportunity lies in selling," he says.

- *Take a gradual entry approach.* Depending on your trading capital, you may want to ease your way into a position. For a typical trader, this tactic may call for you to buy anywhere between 500 and 1000 shares of a stock. With this approach, you can curtail your risk if the stock goes south. And if the stock is doing well or is in the beginning stages of an upswing, you can always buy another 1000 shares or so.

- *Avoid stocks that are thinly traded or have low volume.* The exact amount of volume a direct access trader scans the market for is partly contingent on his or her risk-reward ratio and trading capital. Very active online traders, however, typically look for volume of at least 100,000 shares. By trading exclusively in volatile stocks, traders can obtain the price movement and liquidity they need to get in and out of the market fast.

- *Never place a market order for a stock at the opening of the market.* During the first 10 minutes of a trading day, the price of a stock can be boosted by different factors—including trading of that issue in the overnight session or pre-opening bell good news. In either scenario, if you place a market order at the opening, you basically would be ensuring that you pay the highest possible price for that stock.

- *Maintain your capital.* There may come a time when the upside of a trade looks very good, but it would require you to take on unprecedented risk. In this scenario, it is wiser to take the safer approach and skip the trade. There always will be the opportunity to snag more profits, but if you lose a serious portion of your capital, your trading career could be brought to an abrupt end.

- *Trade smaller amounts of shares when you are experiencing problems.* Being hit with multiple losses can be overwhelming, so you should ease off the throttle a bit when you hit a rough patch of trades. Scaling back on your average share size not only can help you minimize risk but also can ease your anxiety level. Traders with less experience should pay particular attention to this guideline.

- *Take all of your trades and dissect them at the end of the trading day.* By figuring out what you did right, what you did wrong, and what you should have done differently, you will provide yourself with a roadmap for success in future trades.

- *Create a set of written goals.* Lastly, by writing down what you hope to accomplish, you can objectively evaluate the results you have achieved and the progress you need to make. "Those goals will change over time, but it is very important that you have a way to motivate yourself and measure yourself by looking at those goals," says Abell. "If you're not going to do this, I think you're putting yourself at risk again."

3

BUILDING YOUR ELECTRONIC TRADING PORTFOLIO

Depending on your trading capital and tolerance for loss, you may prefer one electronic trading strategy above all others. Sometimes, however, your favorite strategy may not be working, and unless you want to be stuck in mud, you have to adopt a different technique. Remember, the market is constantly evolving, and consequently, at times you will have to take a "road less traveled" to achieve positive results.

In this chapter we are going to outline a variety of direct access trading strategies—including scalping, momentum trading, and swing trading. To get a feel for when to use these strategies, you must first understand the criteria that drive the traders who employ them. This is why we will discuss, among other things, the average price increment used by a scalper, the risk-reward ratio of a typical momentum player, and the average length of time a swing trader holds a position. Moreover, we will unveil the types of stocks that are best suited for each different strategy and explore the pros and cons of a nonconventional trading technique known as *short selling.*

Of course, to make use of any direct access trading strategy, you have to be able to read and evaluate Nasdaq level II—the dynamically updating quote screen that shows all the top bids and offers for a stock. We will walk you through level II and then move on to examine order-routing choices and execution destinations.

After you determine the quote you want to chase with the help of level II, you then must figure out whether you are going to route your order to an electronic communication network (ECN) or a market maker. Most of the direct access systems provide direct electronic connectivity to a bevy of ECNs. However, if you want to route an order to a market maker, you have to go through either SelectNet or the Small Order Execution System (SOES)—the Nasdaq's order entry and execution systems.

Choosing the right order-routing path is especially important for direct access traders because this choice could very well determine whether you get speedy executions and complete fills. Thus we will take a close look at the benefits of each of the three different order-routing methods.

Quite often, direct access trading can seem very confusing—especially when it comes to assimilating information about order-routing systems, execution destinations, and Nasdaq level II. In addition, truth be told, the only way you are going to truly understand how all this works is through real-world trading experience. The descriptions and advice laid out in the rest of this chapter, however, should at least get you headed in the right direction.

NASDAQ LEVEL II

As we have already noted, Nasdaq level II displays, in real time, all the best bids and offers for a given stock—regardless of whether these quotes come from ECNs or market makers. The left-hand side of the level II window displays the best buy orders (bids), whereas the right-hand side shows the best sell orders (offers). Each bid and offer contains the name of market maker or ECN that is placing the quote, the quote itself, and the number of shares the market maker or ECN is willing to fill.

The inside bid and inside offer are displayed at the top of the left- and right-hand column, respectively. Various bits of information are listed above these columns, including the identity of the stock, the total volume the stock has generated for the day, the intraday high and low for the stock, and the amount of points the stock has advanced or declined since the opening bell.

On top of interpreting information when eyeing level II, a trader also typically takes a peek at the time and sales report for a stock. This report, which is usually located adjacent to level II on the right-hand side, chronologically lists the prices and sizes of all the trades that actually have been executed for a stock during the course of a day. Knowing the time and sales information is important, says Ken Johnson, chief executive officer of sixthmarket.com, because it gives you a clue about the direction in which you should be leaning. "If [the stock] is getting executed over toward the bid, then I know a lot of people are selling into the market. If it's getting executed [more toward] the offer, then I know that a lot of people are buying from the market makers, . . . and the price is liable to go up," says Johnson.

Meanwhile, via Nasdaq level II, an individual investor can keep a close eye on the price movements of different market makers and ECNs. By doing so, an investor can learn to accurately predict the direction in which a stock is going to move—especially if he or she understands the strategies used by the market makers who trade that stock most actively.

Unfortunately, however, starting with the inception of the order handling rules in January 1997, it has become increasingly difficult to read the moves of market makers. The rules stated that market makers were required to publicly display a minimum share size of 100 for each stock they traded. Prior to the launch of the rules, however, market makers were required to publicly post a minimum of 1000 shares for every stock in which they made a market. In other words, if a market maker displayed his or her desire to sell stock XYZ at 49¾, then he or she had to say that he or she was willing to fill at least 1000 shares at that price. And if you were the first in line to take this offer, the market maker was obligated to fill your order for 1000 shares at 49¾.

"Every time . . . [a market maker] would jump to the bid, in the old days, you would buy. . . . You'd take it up a half and you'd get out, and that was the secret of scalping," says Johnson. "You could make eight trades in a day and make a half on all of them—just by following Goldman [Sachs]. Now, you don't see that that much, because they just don't telegraph the same way that they used to."

Indeed, after the rules were implemented, many market makers started to display 100 shares—the minimum they were obligated to post. And to this day, if you look at a level II window, you will see lots of market maker bids and offers for just 100 shares. Consequently, the ECNs have become a very important liquidity mechanism for individual investors. "The most important thing I look at [on level II] is where the ECNs are, because that's where the liquidity is right now. Every now and then, you will see a bona fide Nasdaq market maker . . . post some size out there. But most of the time they hide behind the order handling rules and post 100 shares so that you never know what kind of liquidity they've got," says Johnson.

ECNS: KINGS OF LIQUIDITY

After interpreting the ECN and market maker quotes displayed on level II, you must then decide what kind of order you want to place and where, exactly, you want to send that order. Most direct access systems provide you with three order-routing options: SOES, SelectNet, and direct ECN access. With both SOES and SelectNet, you can route orders to market makers—and SelectNet also offers you the ability to preference an ECN. However, both systems have glitches and, most significantly, are at least a couple of steps slower than using a direct link to an ECN.

Through SOES, individual investors can route orders to market makers—who have the exclusive right to view and respond to orders. However, market makers cannot use SOES to execute their own orders, and the system has a maximum order size of 1000 shares.

SelectNet, on the other hand, has no order size limit. Moreover, through the so-called SelectNet Preference version of the system, you can send an order not only to a specific market maker but also to your ECN of choice. On the down side, however, after you place your order on SelectNet, you cannot cancel it for at least 10 seconds—a time span that can feel like an eternity to rapid-fire scalpers.

In the not-too-distant future, Nasdaq plans to replace its outdated SOES systems with a single platform dubbed *SuperSOES*. However, taking all the current facts into consideration, Johnson says that direct connectivity to ECNs is the best order-routing option for direct access traders.[1] "If I want to get in or out of a stock, I look for an ECN showing the most size, and I go and hit them directly," he says.

On average, the ECNs—which account for more than 30 percent of Nasdaq's total volume—post larger bids and offers on level II than do market makers. Whereas market makers often post 100 shares, says Johnson, ECNs usually display at least 1000 shares. Translation: ECNs usually provide more liquidity. And the more liquid the execution destination, the better is the chance that your incoming order will be matched.

What is more, frequently, the ECNs display superior prices to market makers. Thus ECNs give traders the best odds of getting complete fills at a fair price.

As of this writing, there were nine ECNs, but only two of them—Reuters' Instinet Corp. and Datek Online Holdings' Island—were dominant. According to a report by Celent Communications, Instinet and Island recorded 58 and 21 percent of the total ECN volume in 1999, respectively.[2] Moreover, Johnson says that since they have the most liquidity, these equity trade-matching systems are the players that direct access traders should be watching most closely on level II.

Besides keeping an eye on what Instinet and Island are doing on level II, it also makes sense, if you have the resources, to obtain access to the complete order books of these ECN giants. With level II, you can only see the best bid or best offer Instinet and Island have posted for a stock. However, if you can tap into their books, you can see all the bids and offers these ECNs have for a specific stock. As a result, you will be able to see exactly where the support level is for that stock. "If you can go out and look at the depth of the Instinet book or the depth of the Island book, you're getting a much better picture of where the market is, . . . [and that's] more important than, for example, what Goldman is doing with their 100 shares," says Johnson.

This said—and the importance of Instinet and Island notwithstanding—a direct access trader also should keep track of the progress smaller and midsize ECNs are making. In a relatively short time period, the landscape can change, and in turn, you may have to rethink your execution strategy. In fact, a couple of the midsized ECNs are beginning to challenge Island for its ranking as the second-largest ECN—in terms of average daily volume.[3]

SCALPING AND DE FACTO MARKET MAKING

The rise of ECNs has been particularly beneficial to one active group of traders—the scalpers. *Scalping,* which requires extremely fast decision-making skills, takes place when a trader attempts to snatch small profits from minuscule intraday price fluctuations in a stock. Often, a scalper will be in and out of a single stock several times during the course of a day, hoping to make $150 here and $200 there. Although this may not seem like much, these small profits can really add up, because the average scalper makes between 50 and 250 trades per day,

Scalpers are usually looking to trade high-volume, low-volatility stocks. The average price fluctuation of a stock can be just a "teenie"— as long as there is enough activity for the scalper to consistently trade that stock. After all, consistency is really the name of the game for the scalper, who must have a very good ratio of winning versus losing positions to produce significant profits.

To generate such profits, you also must trade larger amounts of shares than you would if you were, say, a momentum trader. Since you are trading in such small increments, you must be willing to pony up 2000 shares (or more) to make some decent money. In addition, since you are playing for a diminutive upside, you must use "very aggressive" protective stops to keep your losses as small as possible, says Johnson. In line with this thinking, if you are on the long side of a trade, you constantly must be on the lookout for any kind of pullback against your position. Quickly recognizing a pullback will enable you to expeditiously exit a trade and minimize your loss.

Most of the time, whether they are exiting a losing trade or locking in profits on a winner, scalpers send their orders directly to an ECN. Johnson says that since market makers are not posting a lot of size on Nasdaq level II, ECNs are now the only true source of liquidity for individual investors. Therefore, he says, you have to be a "terrific ECN player" to be a good scalper. And to be a superior ECN player, you have to be using a sophisticated system that provides direct connectivity to ECNs.

However, just because you use a direct access system that is reliable and fast does not mean that you will have an easy time scalping. Howard Abell, cofounder of invest2know.com, says that it is hard to scalp today because it is difficult to interpret the moves of market makers. "In the past, if you had a stock with a ⅛ spread, you'd know what your risk is, because if the levels on the bid were deep enough, you could buy stock, and if you were wrong, you could get out right away," he notes. In contrast, in today's market, if you buy 1000 shares, you cannot bail out of a stock as quickly because there are not enough sizable bids in the stock, says Abell.

Before the order handling rules, says Johnson, scalping was relatively easy, because every time a market maker made a move in a security, he or she was putting 2000 shares (1000 on the bid side and 1000 on the offer side) "on the line." In fact, he says, he used to teach his direct access students to scalp because it was the strategy that provided them with the greatest chance for success. But now, because of the reduction in market maker liquidity, Johnson discourages his students from trying to make a living through scalping.

This said, Johnson concedes that he has friends who are "fabulous" scalpers. What's more, to get them use to buying and selling stocks in a lightning-quick fashion, Johnson says he instructs each of his students to make 10 "flat" scalp trades of 100 shares each. "What you're trying to instill in people is that speed counts and that you can get in and get out without getting yourself killed," says Johnson.

The great speed with which scalpers trade gives them one distinct advantage: the ability to exploit the bid/ask spread. Like market makers, some scalpers buy on the bid and sell on the offer—snatching profits from the difference between the two quotes. "Individual investors are now able to use direct access technology to actually trade [a stock] as a competitive market maker," says All-Tech Direct's Harvey Houtkin. "If there's a stock with a 1/8-point spread that is trading on both the bid and offer side, you can sit there all day long and make teenies and 1/8s . . . and nickels and dimes all day long when we go to decimals. And the stock won't have to move at all."

Houtkin, however, is not fond of labeling traders who buy on the bid and sell on the offer as scalpers. Instead, he describes them as "de facto market makers." "I wouldn't call this scalping. Is a retail store scalping if they buy something wholesale and sell it retail? What you're doing is basically supplying liquidity and getting paid for it. You're buying on the bid side and selling on the offer side, to the extent that you can, and you're also mixing in momentum techniques," he says.

Traders who act as "de facto market makers," says Houtkin, are in a good position to succeed—in part because they have absolutely no "emotional attachment" to a stock. "You're committing capital by buying inventory and then looking to immediately turn over that inventory. That's significantly different from investing in a company because you think the stock will do exceptionally well," he says.

MOMENTUM AND SWING TRADING

Dissimilar to scalpers, momentum traders and swing traders often are looking to make a sizable gain per trade. The gain desired varies with each individual trader, but on average, these two groups of traders are looking to make at least ½ point. Also, unlike scalpers, the momentum players and swing traders are trading in wider time frames. In the case of momentum players, they hold an open position anywhere from a few minutes to a few hours—and may even take home a position overnight on occasion. Swing traders, on the other hand, typically maintain their positions anywhere from 1 to 5 days.

As part of their high-risk, high-reward strategy, momentum players tend to trade high-volatility stocks—including technology stocks, sector-leading stocks, and stocks that have made news. They determine whether a stock is in motion, in part, by keeping one eye trained on the market makers and the other on the time and sales report.

Since their risk is so high, momentum traders will at times try to scale out of positions—incrementally locking in portions of profits at different price points. By doing so, they can both retain their profits and protect themselves against big losses.

Minimizing risk, not surprisingly, is also near the top of the agenda of swing traders. Abell says that swing traders who orchestrate trades based on trends and trend reversals they see in specific stocks and the overall market must live by a couple of rules: Do not overpay for stocks when you are looking to make a "½ point or a point," and use market orders when you need to drop a losing trade. "If the market is going against you and you need to get out, you get out at the market (via a market order). You should only get out via limit orders in a profitable situation," he says. Abell, who describes himself as a "pattern trader," says he uses market orders 60 percent of the time.

Peter Sweeney, a direct access swing trader from Connecticut, also uses market orders quite frequently. If he is looking to "pick a bottom" to buy a stock, Sweeney says, he will use a limit order. But most of the time he will input a market order. "If a stock has been consolidating below a trend line that I have drawn, I'm looking to buy that stock when it breaks up through that trend line," he says. "When it does break, if I'm right, many times it runs real fast. And if I wait to try and screw with buying it for an ⅛ or ¹⁄₁₆ cheaper [via a limit order], I miss it."

Frequently, a swing trader looks at different charts to determine a stock's resistance and support levels. The *resistance point, or ceiling,* is the price above which a stock has not traded historically. The *support level,* in contrast, is the price below which a declining stock has not faded historically. In other words, if you had a stock with an intraday resistance of 80 and an intraday support of 70, once the stock reached 80, it probably would take a downward turn, and once it reached 70, it likely would rise up. Through evaluating a stock's resistance and support, you can get a pretty fair idea about where you should enter and exit a trade.

Speaking of entering a stock, Sweeney says that one of his favorite times to buy is when a stock has broken through its 52-week resistance level toward the close of the market. If a stock achieves its 52-week high near 4 P.M. EST, he says, it will be fueled by after hours chat room hype and likely gap up anywhere from 10 to 20 percent the next morning. "If anything, it's the greater fool theory. . . . You know the stock is going to the moon, so get on board," says Sweeney. Therefore, he says, it is a wise move to buy that stock immediately after it breaks through its resistance and then sell it near the opening the next day.

BETTING ON A DECLINE

Most of the time, traders buy a stock at a quote they perceive as cheap and then sell it after it has shot up to a price that meets or exceeds their profit expectations. In this buy-low, sell-high process—also known as *longing a stock*—the trader anticipates that a security will increase in value at some point after his or her initial purchase.

However, at the opposite end of the spectrum there also lies a more infrequently used strategy known as *short selling*. Simply put, traders who short stocks are borrowing shares to sell a stock in anticipation that the stock is going to take a dive. Technically speaking, if you engage in short selling, you are actually agreeing to borrow the shares from your broker's clearing arm. The catch? You must buy back the number of shares you borrowed somewhere down the road. Ideally, however, you will make a sizable profit by buying back the stock at a significantly cheaper price than the price at which you sold it.

For instance, you may borrow shares to short a stock at 48 in anticipation that it will fall all the way down to 40. Then, if the stock does indeed fall to 40, you buy back the shares you borrowed to fulfill—or cover—your shorting obligation. "Then you've done a buy and a sell and made 8 points. . . . It's just that you've reversed the [normal trading] timing," says Johnson.

In order to short a stock, you have to first open a margin account with your brokerage firm. When you open a margin account, Johnson explains, one of the things you are signing is a document that says you will allow your broker's clearing arm to use securities you hold as collateral for your margin loans. Your broker, as a result, has protection if you rack up losses—either while shorting or going long—that you do not have enough cash to pay for immediately.

Where, you may ask, do these shares you are borrowing when you are shorting a stock come from? Well, when you open a margin account—in addition to providing your broker with collateral in case you lose your shirt—you are empowering the broker's clearing affiliate with the right to "loan your shares" to another investor, says Johnson.

As long as you have the collateral in your account to cover any losses that you incur, you are not committed to any time frame when you short a stock. That really depends on your trading style.

If you are a scalper, for example, you are looking to book lots of small profits on a rapid-fire basis—and therefore you may want to wait only a few seconds before you cover your short. A swing trader, on the other hand, may want to maintain his or her short positions for a couple of hours—and, in certain situations, even a couple of days. However, if you are going to hold on to a short overnight, just remember that the longer you keep that position open, the more risk you are going to have to assume.

Moreover, if you are planning to hold a short overnight, you also must be wary of the moves of market makers toward the close of the market. During a down day in the market, the market makers may start buying a stock as it inches toward the close, hoping to send individual investors who hold short positions in that stock into a state of panic. Known as a *short squeeze,* this strategy—in which market makers intentionally drive up the price of a stock—is intended to entice individuals to cover their shorts. All the covers, of course, would rally the price of the stock—and once they believe that they have forced all the amateurs to buy back the shares they borrowed, the market makers could then short the stock themselves. Thus, do not forget to take extra caution when you are holding a short heading into the close.

Although it may sound more complex than a traditional buy transaction, if you are using a sophisticated direct access system, the actual process of shorting a stock is seamless to a trader. In fact, all you do is bang out a couple of keystrokes, and your system automatically tells you if the stock has shares available for borrowing. "Our computer does all the work for the trader. It has a vast list of all the stocks that are available [for borrowing]. If it's available, it lets you short it. If it's not available, it says 'No!' " says All-Tech's Houtkin.

Most often, a short sell will occur when a trader notices a couple of different "bearish patterns" in the marker, says Abell. A trader's list of candidates for a short sell, he says, usually comprises the weakest performing stocks in different sectors. On any given day, the worst performing stock in the biotechnology sector, for example, could be a candidate for a short sell. "I sell weakness and buy strength in terms of the relative strength of the stocks that I'm looking at," says Abell. "I look at the tone of the market. . . . If the tone of the market is weak, it's very difficult to pick out one or two or three stocks that are going to defy the market and go up significantly. So you either step back or you try to participate in a weak market [via a short sell]."

Active short selling in a weak market, says Houtkin, is an advanced technique that typically is employed only by "more sophisticated" traders. Beyond knowing what signs to watch for, there is also a psychological barrier that traders must hurdle if they are going to short. "Most normal people feel that selling something you don't own is inherently wrong," explains Houtkin. However, he says that traders must find a way to get past their fears, because knowing how to short can be your best—and sometimes only—path to profit on days when the market is caught in a downward spiral.

NOTES

1. Sang Lee, Octavio Marenzi, and Jody Cornish, Profiling the ECNs, Celent Communications, www.celent.com, Figure 23, p. 36.

2. Celent Communications, Figure 22, p. 35.

3. Celent Communications, Figure 23, p. 36.

C H A P T E R

SUPERSOES: THE ORDER EXECUTION EQUALIZER?

Historically speaking, from a direct access trader's perspective, Nasdaq's order delivery and execution systems could best be described as flawed. Operating separately, both SelectNet and the Small Order Execution System (SOES) have in the past been driven by rules that provided market makers with an unfair advantage over direct access traders who routed orders through those networks.

Moreover—due in part to the fact that Nasdaq's use of multiple execution systems potentially could expose them to double executions—market makers traditionally have not been inclined to post larger-sized orders on Nasdaq level II. And, of course, the less size market makers display, the more difficult it is to analyze the direction in which the "big boys" are taking a stock.

However, as of November 20, 2000, Nasdaq planned to implement an enhanced order execution network that could alter the direct access trader–market maker relationship significantly. The new system, dubbed *SuperSOES,* is expected eventually to replace both SOES and SelectNet as Nasdaq's execution pipeline for all market maker–addressed orders. Under Nasdaq's grand plan, instead of using their front-end direct access software to send a smaller order (through SOES) or a larger order (via SelectNet) to a market maker for execution, direct access traders will have to use SuperSOES to trade electronically with market makers.

Following the launch of SuperSOES, SelectNet essentially will be transformed into an indications of interest (IOI) system, through which market participants can communicate their desire to buy or sell a stock at different price and size levels. From a technical standpoint, Nasdaq officials say that SelectNet will become a "nonliability order delivery and negotiation system." In plain English, this means that any market maker who receives a SelectNet-delivered order will no longer be required to execute that order. Rather, the market maker will be able to choose whether he or she wants to execute the order.

However, since SelectNet orders will no longer be subject to firm quote rule obligations, it is likely that very few direct access traders will use SelectNet to route orders to market makers in the future. In fact, Nasdaq officials expect SuperSOES to capture all the daily executions currently performed by SelectNet (700,000 as of July 2000) and SOES (124,000) combined.

While SelectNet is essentially being removed from the market maker execution equation, it will continue to operate as a conduit for direct access traders who wish to route orders to electronic communication networks (ECNs) via a nondirect mechanism. "The ECNs will still be accessible, like they are today, via SelectNet, . . . [so the ECNs] can still drive the inside quote," notes William Broka, senior vice president of trading and market services at Nasdaq.

ECNs, as we documented earlier in this book, really started to emerge after the January 1997 rollout of the Securities and Exchange Commission's order handling rules. However, the histories of SOES and SelectNet actually date back much further than this. SOES, introduced in 1984, was designed to give small retail investors—trading orders of 1000 shares or fewer—access to the best prices available on Nasdaq. In contrast, SelectNet made its debut in 1990, targeting investors who wanted an electronic mechanism for trading larger-sized orders.

Prior to the launch of the order handling rules, SOES was the system of choice for many individual investors who traded on behalf of their own accounts—partly because market makers, in accordance with a National Association of Securities Dealers (NASD) rule, were required to publicly display 1000 shares for most of the stocks they traded through SOES. Shortly after implementation of the rules, however, the NASD amended this rule, stating that a market maker had to publicly display a minimum of only 100 shares for each stock he or she traded through SOES.

After this rule change took place, it became more difficult to read the moves of market makers, says Harvey Houtkin, chairman and chief executive officer of All-Tech Direct, an electronic day trading firm that owns the Attain ECN. Unfortunately, he says, the practice of market makers displaying 100-share orders on level II has become all too common. "Now, basically, market makers have no obligation to show size," he laments.

However, the new SuperSOES platform will bring with it some rule changes that may entice market makers to display greater size on Nasdaq level II. Specifically, SuperSOES is expected to

- Increase the maximum size order of SOES from 1000 to 1 million shares.
- Allow market makers to trade on behalf of their own accounts.
- Eradicate market maker dual liability concerns.
- Reduce or eliminate the time interval market makers have to execute consecutive same-priced orders.

Beyond providing some more incentives for market makers to display greater size, SuperSOES also should limit the ability of market makers to effectively hold a stock hostage at a specific price level. However, while the direct access trading community could certainly reap some benefits from SuperSOES, the system will not be without its share of stumbling blocks.

For example, direct access traders who send their orders through SuperSOES will be competing head-on for executions with other market markers. And since competition is expected to be more fierce on SuperSOES than it ever was on SOES, direct access orders sometimes may get stuck in the SuperSOES queue. In the rest of this chapter, in the name of the direct access trader, we will explore the pros and cons of SuperSOES.

SIZE MATTERS

Originally, Nasdaq was supposed to have SuperSOES up and running by the spring of 2000. It missed that date, however, and then whiffed on another projected rollout date in the summer—before finally settling on November.

While conceding that Nasdaq missed its first two scheduled SuperSOES installation dates (in May and July), Broka says that Nasdaq decided to delay the launch of the system only after market makers, ECNs, and order-entry firms pointed out the inherent flaws in Super-SOES. "They wanted us to make a couple of adjustments to make this system more effective," he says.

One of the changes market participants requested was an increase in the maximum order size of SuperSOES. Originally, Nasdaq said it was going to put a cap of 9900 shares per order entered on SuperSOES—a significant jump from the 1000-share limit that SOES participants are subject to today. However, this plan was scrapped when some market participants complained—loudly—that the 9900-share limit was too restrictive.

These market participants argued that orders could get stuck in the queue if an investor had to, for example, enter two separate orders to grab all 11,000 shares of a bid or an offer a market maker was displaying publicly. Such inefficiencies, they asserted, could have a negative impact on both individual investors and professional traders.

Subsequently, Nasdaq decided to boost the SuperSOES maximum order size to 999,999 shares. As a result, Nasdaq officials expect to see more and more market participants entering larger-sized orders into SuperSOES. "This does eliminate the cap we had on order entry. . . . You're going to have the flexibility to route orders for 2000 or 6000 shares or whatever," says Broka. "That's a positive, I think, for anyone who wants to deal in size in our market."

However, just because direct access traders will be able to route larger-sized orders through SuperSOES does not necessarily mean that those orders will get filled. "Remember, you can still only execute against whatever is being shown by the market makers [on Nasdaq level II]. . . . You can send a large order into SuperSOES, but that doesn't mean that there will be anybody on the other side of it," says Townsend Analytics president and cofounder, Stuart Townsend.

Still, while there is no disputing this statement, it is also true that SuperSOES will provide market makers with more incentives to display size than SOES did. In the past, for example, market makers were only able to use SOES to fill customer limit orders. Under SuperSOES, however, market makers will be free to trade on behalf of their own proprietary accounts.

This fact, says an executive at a day trading firm, should "go a long way toward resolving the problem" of market makers not reflecting size. "Now that they're able to use SOES to trade on behalf of their own accounts, the true market makers will be showing size, because they'll be SOESing each other," the executive predicts.

However, the executive also concedes that allowing market makers to execute proprietary trades over SuperSOES could have some negative competitive ramifications for direct access traders—particularly for the smaller traders who typically trade fewer than 1000 shares. "The fact that you're now going to be competing against professional traders and market makers for the same liquidity [over SuperSOES] could be somewhat of a disadvantage," the executive says.

While lauding the enhancements Nasdaq has made to its new order execution network, Nasdaq's Broka concurs that it may at times be more difficult for direct access traders to get their orders executed over SuperSOES than it was for them to perform trades through SOES. Since SuperSOES will be open to "bids and offers from all market participants," Broka says that it is likely that Nasdaq's order execution network will have "more orders in the queue than there are today." However, he also emphasizes that SuperSOES could end up making stock sizes more transparent by eliminating the need for market makers to worry about dual liability.

In the pre-SuperSOES realm, market makers faced the possibility of simultaneously receiving orders from both SelectNet and SOES. Because SelectNet is being transformed into a nonliability system, however, market makers will no longer have to worry about filling dual orders simultaneously. Consequently, says Broka, more and more market makers may be "encouraged" to publicly display larger size.

"A lot of firms [today] are showing 100 shares because they are exposed to both a SelectNet and a SOES execution at the same time," says Broka. "[But] we are going to eliminate dual liability, and that may encourage the display of greater size . . . because you can only have one execution, versus the two you may have to fill today as a market maker."

Indeed, the executive at the day trading firm says the main reason Nasdaq is getting rid of SelectNet is because many larger market makers were upset about the whole dual liability issue. "What was happening was they would get accessed on SelectNet, and someone else would be hitting them on SOES simultaneously. And they'd be filling two orders, though they were really only obligated to fill one," he says.

Despite the fact that it will provide market makers with the ability to perform proprietary trading and eliminate dual liability, Houtkin does not expect the launch of SuperSOES to spur market makers to display more size. "Market makers never want to display size, because they figure, if you don't display size, you don't commit yourself to a firm transaction. And if you don't commit yourself to a firm transaction, you have a lot of wiggle room not to do a trade. You just put out an order for 100 shares, and that way, you can just play with an order based on who's sending you an order," explains Houtkin.

Thanks at least in part to the payment for order flow arrangements we discussed earlier in this book, Houtkin says, market makers do not have to worry about receiving an influx of orders. In fact, Houtkin says that some market makers reason that if they are going to pay to receive order flow from an online discount broker, then why should they tip their hand by displaying larger size? "Knight Trimark, for example, pays off half the free world to get order flow. They don't want to compete on price or size—they want to compete on payoff," says Houtkin. "They want as little size showing as possible, so that if there's a sell order, they can trade it down. And if there's a buy order, they can take it up."

However, one stock regulatory official says that Houtkin's size complaints are completely self-serving. "What he's basically saying is that the market makers aren't standing up so that [day traders] can bang away at them," says the official, noting that day traders have "zero obligation" with regard to showing size.

Prior to 1997, market makers, in accordance with an NASD rule, were required to publicly display 1000 shares for most of the stocks they traded through SOES. Moreover, they were required to provide a fill for whatever size they displayed. Thus, conceivably, a market maker could have received a customer limit order for 500 shares at a specific price but have been forced to display 1000 shares (and, in turn, provide a 1000-share fill).

Shortly after the order handling rules took effect, however, the NASD reduced its minimum size requirements for market makers via its so-called actual size rule. The actual size rule, which was approved by the Securities and Exchange Commission (SEC), stipulated that market makers were required to publicly display a minimum of only 100 shares for each stock they traded.

This size reduction, says a regulatory official, was intended to help market makers control their risk. "That's at the heart of the actual size rule. . . . Instead of being hit for 1000, 1000, 1000, you are hit for whatever quote size you display," he says. "The great debate was, Would people be willing to compete on the basis of size? And there are some market makers that are in [SOES] for some size, but most of them are not."

The official says that for many markets makers who traded through SOES, displaying 100 shares was merely a way for them to reduce their risk. Houtkin, however, describes SOES as "the biggest farce ever" and says the changes that are being incorporated into SuperSOES are nothing to write home about. "Now [Nasdaq is] trying to do what it should have done to begin with," he says. "We've been asking for that for 12 years. It should be a bigger size, and everyone should be allowed to use it."

What's more, everyone who uses SuperSOES should be entitled to speedy executions. However, noting that Nasdaq's track record with order delivery and execution systems is poor, Townsend says that execution speed is one potential area of weakness for SuperSOES. Indeed, Townsend—who owns and operates the RealTick direct access system and also owns a minority stake in the Archipelago ECN—does not believe SuperSOES will hold great appeal for market makers.

"Nasdaq clearly believes that they will receive more order flow. . . . [But] we think there is a distinct probability that SuperSOES will reduce order flow to Nasdaq," says Townsend. "It's going to be so bad that the ECNs will be the primary beneficiary, and even more trades will be done through ECNs."

SuperSOES, he says, is bound to experience a "slowdown." And rather than risk getting bogged down, market makers could turn to ECNs. Under the order handling rules, Townsend points out, market makers have the option of passing on unwanted customer limit orders to ECNs.

Specifically, Townsend illuminates the limit order rule, which applies to orders of 10,000 shares or fewer, and states that a market maker who receives a limit order priced better than his or her own public quote has three options: execute the order, display the order, or reroute the order to an ECN. If SuperSOES experiences any execution or display meltdowns, says Townsend, the ECN option should become particularly appealing to market makers.

This said, all the direct access vendors, including Townsend Analytics, are adjusting their trading systems to account for Nasdaq's execution consolidation. In Townsend's case, instead of having the ability to transact with market makers via both SOES and SelectNet, clients of RealTick will now have only one option (SuperSOES) for executing trades with market makers. "We will have a link to SuperSOES . . . that will work much the same way SOES does today," says Townsend. In addition, for its clients who want access to an indirect vehicle for sending orders to ECNs, RealTick also will continue to provide an interface to SelectNet.

TIME CHANGE

Whether you are talking about SelectNet or SOES, time has always been an issue. For direct access traders, one of the potential danger areas of SelectNet is a rule that stipulates that once you enter an order into the network, you cannot cancel that order for at least 10 seconds. Omar Amanat, chief executive officer of Tradescape.com—a direct access broker that also owns the MarketXT ECN—says that the 10-second rule was troublesome because it allowed market makers to manipulate orders coming from the retail investor community.

"Once you send an order through SelectNet, market makers are literally able to capture and hold your order, and then determine for 10 seconds (and in some cases 20 seconds, depending on the latency of the message traffic), . . . whether or not they want to fill that order," says Amanat. "This is like having a free ticket. They can decide what they want to do with that order over a period of 10 seconds. And in an extremely volatile market, the market may move $3/8$ of 3 points within those 10 or 20 seconds."

However, once SelectNet gets transitioned into a nonliability system, the 10-second rule should cease to be an issue for direct access traders. Of course, this does not mean that direct access traders who are routing orders through Nasdaq's technology will never again have to worry about execution delays. SOES, just like its sister network, has had its share of time-delay controversies.

Most significantly, under the old SOES network, there was one rule that allotted market makers a 17-second interval to execute against consecutive same-priced orders. For example, if a market maker was showing 1000 shares at a 10 bid and a market sell order for 500 shares comes in and hits that bid, through SOES, then that market maker would have 17 seconds before he or she was responsible for getting rid of his or her remaining 500 shares. In other words, in this scenario, a market maker who remained at his or her same 10 bid could not get hit for the leftover shares until 17 seconds had elapsed.

Under SuperSOES, however, this 17-second interval will be reduced significantly. In fact, in the case of very liquid stocks such as Microsoft, Dell, and Amazon.com, the interval will be eliminated all together. "We're going to a variable timer in there so that in certain stocks there will be no delay between order delivery against the same market maker at the same price level," says Nasdaq's Broka.

Not surprisingly, in the past, some market makers took advantage of SOES by selling off the shares they had in 100-share increments 17 seconds apart. "What these guys would do is that they would sell 100 shares and then stay at that price, and then sell another 100 shares," says Houtkin. "Let's say, for example, a stock was offered at 20, and the market maker stayed at 20, got SOESed, and did 100 shares. Then [he or she would] stay there for another 17 seconds, and do another 100 shares. In the meantime, because of the fast speed markets move at today, the prices below your [order] would all disappear."

If it works as planned, however, the variable time should help level the playing field for retail investors. Initially, the NASD decided that the time interval would be reduced to 5 seconds for all Nasdaq stocks market makers traded through SuperSOES. After receiving input from various market participants, however, Nasdaq scrapped this idea. "That [5-second interval] was fine in certain stocks, but to have that apply across the board to all stocks—particularly the most active and most liquid stocks—wasn't fair," says Broka. "Many people were concerned that this would hold up executions in the marketplace for an unreasonable period of time."

Indeed, Townsend says that unless there were "a lot of market makers at the inside quote," SuperSOES's 5-second interval could have led to "significant" execution delays. "If there is only one [market maker] at that price, that means that stock is frozen for 5 seconds. And that's an eternity in the [Nasdaq] market," he says.

Taking such complaints to heart, the NASD eventually decided to eliminate the time interval for the "top 100 or 200" Nasdaq stocks, says Broka. "If there happens to be a single market maker at the best bid or best offer, and they get hit for 100 shares and have 900 shares remaining, we don't want to hold the market up for 5 seconds before we process the next order [for a highly active stock]," he says.

At the opposite end of the spectrum, market makers definitely will be afforded a time delay when they are trading the least liquid Nasdaq stocks through SuperSOES. Without providing a lot specifics, Broka says that the least liquid stocks will have a delay of "more than 5 seconds," the most actively traded stocks will have no delay, and some stocks in between will be subject to a 5-second delay.

Broka also emphasizes that any time a market maker gets filled for all his or her shares, the time delay rule no longer applies. If, for instance, a market maker is showing 100 shares at a 20 bid and a market sell order for 100 shares comes in and hits that 20 bid, then the market maker's size goes from 100 to 0, and the time delay is voided. In such a scenario, a market maker would have two choices: He or she could either refresh his or her size at the same price or move his or her market to a different price. Either way, though, he or she would not have the luxury of a time interval. "If [that market maker] is next in line to get hit, he [or she] gets hit," says Broka.

Although there are differences of opinion on the degree to which the SuperSOES time interval alteration will affect direct access traders, most industry observers agree that it should prove beneficial. "Now, market makers are not going to be able to . . . [display] consecutive 100 share orders and, at each interval, hold up the market for 17 seconds," says the executive at the day trading firm. "This will hopefully make the markets move [with] more fluidity."

THE NEW SELECTNET

Similarly, the consolidation of two Nasdaq order execution systems into one is also expected to add to the fluidity of the market. In the past, orders sent to market makers through SelectNet were subject to firm quote obligations—meaning that market makers were responsible for executing them. Following the launch of SuperSOES, however, market makers will no longer be obligated to fill orders sent to them via SelectNet.

Traders, if they so choose, will have the ability to transmit orders through SelectNet, but only if an order is 100 shares above the share size of the quote to which they are directing their order (which, in effect, eliminates execution liability for the recipient). Collectively, these facts are expected to transform SelectNet into an electronic IOI vehicle. "SelectNet will become strictly a broadcast mechanism that will allow traders to offer stock out—either at the offer or a teenie below the offer or whatever," says Townsend. "You [will] just be advertising to all participants that this is what I have for sale. Whether they choose to take that order will now be their obligation."

Like Townsend, Nasdaq's Broka expects most market participants to use SelectNet as a negotiation mechanism in the future. If, for example, a market maker is showing 1000 shares at 10, he or she can indicate his or her desire to sell 500 shares at 9⅞ through SelectNet. "It's a way for you to advertise an indication of interest and have someone negotiate and respond to you—which is what SelectNet was designed to do in the first place," he says.

SelectNet, Broka points out, also will continue to be the sole order-routing link Nasdaq provides to ECNs. However, will ECNs be flooded with orders from day trading firms, delivered by SelectNet, once SuperSOES is launched? Well, one source worries that dual liability could become an issue for ECNs after SuperSOES makes its debut.

Broka insists, however, that dual liability never has been a problem for ECNs and assures Nasdaq participants that it will continue to be a nonissue in the SuperSOES era. Broka explains that if an ECN matches an order internally while simultaneously receiving an order from SelectNet, that ECN would not be responsible for matching the SelectNet order. "If they're executing an order in their system, it takes their bid or offer out of the market, and they can decline the SelectNet order," he says.

PARTING SHOTS

Despite the potential positive ramifications we have outlined, not everyone in the Nasdaq realm is convinced that SuperSOES will help level the playing field for direct access traders. Don Merz, a direct access trader who trades on behalf of his own account, casts a wary eye toward the alleged benefits of SuperSOES for direct access traders.

It does not make sense for Nasdaq to implement a new execution network, Merz says, unless its big members have pushed for it. And such powerful firms would not be giving SuperSOES the green light if it were not in their own best interests, he theorizes. "With all the smaller people, it's like 'Hey, screw you guys because this is what . . . the big firms want.' That's who Nasdaq gets their money from," he says. "I guess I don't blame them, in a sense, but don't say you're out for the individual and small investors when you're actually out screwing them."

Personally, Merz says, he has not heard a lot of his colleagues complaining abut the current ECN-SelectNet-SOES execution structure for Nasdaq stocks. However, Merz also says that he recognizes that Nasdaq does not particularly care what he thinks, and accordingly, he stands ready for whatever changes the exchange implements. "I don't know how . . .

[SuperSOES is] going to affect anything. All I'm going to do is adapt," he says. "I have to adapt to it . . . [because] that's the only way you survive."

When direct access traders ponder survival, All-Tech's Houtkin says, they should always remember that the Nasdaq is a "dealer-driven market" that was designed to "protect" and benefit the exchange's broker/dealer (i.e., market maker) members. Keeping this in mind, he says, he has no doubt that Nasdaq will "leave in little nuances" in the final version of SuperSOES that will swing the pendulum in the direction of market makers. "Nasdaq will not allow a truly central, competitive, fair, accessible, transparent market," he says. "They will always leave in a few goodies for the boys."

However, despite all his misgivings about the true intentions of Nasdaq, even the ultraskeptical Houtkin says that SuperSOES should provide an upgrade over the exchange's outdated SOES-SelectNet structure. "SuperSOES should have an overall positive effect—I hope," he concludes.

Since SuperSOES will for the first time give marker makers the power to execute proprietary trades, order flow growth could be one result stemming from Nasdaq's rollout of a new execution network. In fact, Nasdaq's Broka expects SuperSOES to generate higher volumes than SelectNet and SOES combined. However, Broka says that he is also not certain that all the changes being incorporated into SuperSOES will lead to greater size transparency on Nasdaq level II.

The day trading executive, meanwhile, believes that SuperSOES will yield positive results for the direct access community. "This will add liquidity to the market. At least, that is what we hope the result will be," he says.

In time, we will be able to judge the true impact of SuperSOES on direct access traders. Regardless of which side of the SuperSOES fence you stand on, however, direct connectivity to ECNs will likely remain the number one order execution choice for direct access traders.

Like its predecessors, the day trading executive says, SuperSOES "won't be nearly as technologically sophisticated" as ECNs. "A system like Island executes a trade in a fraction of a second, in terms of getting a fill and sending back the confirmation," he says. "In contrast, a Nasdaq system [performing the same duties] could take 3 seconds."

5

RISK MANAGEMENT

Recently, when I was sitting in a fast-food restaurant waiting for my take-out order, it started to rain. Even though I knew that the weather forecast for that day had called for cloudy skies with the potential for thunderstorms, I decided to take a gamble and left my umbrella at home.

As I sat in the restaurant, the rain started to pick up a little, transforming from a drizzle to a mild shower. Shortly thereafter, it started coming down in buckets. One minute later, it slowed down to a drizzle again, followed by mild showers, and then—you guessed it—another torrential downpour. Over the course of the next 10 minutes, in front of my disbelieving eyes, the cycle continued: drizzle, hard rain, and downpour; downpour, hard rain, and drizzle.

The rain flows changed rapidly, in a manner that was impossible to predict. It was like nothing I have ever seen or read about—with the exception of the U.S. equity markets. The ebb and flow of U.S. stocks—particularly those listed on the Nasdaq—can change in the blink of an eye. The stocks are extremely volatile and, for the ill-prepared online trader, potentially deadly.

On that day, when I left my apartment—even though I knew of the threat of showers—I took no precautions to protect myself against a rainy day. The odds were against me, but I decided to try to buck them, risking coming home all wet for the reward of not having to carry around an umbrella. What happened? As I sat in the restaurant, I tried to wait until the rain stopped completely. However, after several back-and-forth 3-minute cycles, the rain just got worse, escalating into a fierce storm. Then my patience wore thin, and I decided to try to sprint home. The end result? I wound up getting soaked from head to toe.

Similarly, if you do not craft a trading plan that both protects you against losses and allows you to take advantage of profit opportunities, you could very well end up taking a bath. Obviously, your bath, unlike mine, would be of the figurative kind—as in you will be drenched in losses if you do not employ a sound risk-management strategy.

In case you are not catching my drift, the message here is simple: Managing risk is a never-ending challenge that represents one of the keys to success for direct access traders. Throughout the course of a trading day, you may need to adjust your risk parameters, depending on your current capital situation, the current market trend, and the intraday trend for the stock you are looking to trade. Regardless of what is going on in the market, however, discipline is the key to successful risk management.

In the electronic trading business, there is no room for greed while you are in the money and no room for second guessing while you are losing. Therefore, if and when you adjust your risk-reward ratio, you must be disciplined enough to adhere strictly to your new parameters—particularly your stop loss.

Stop-loss orders, in which traders specify the exact price at which they are looking to exit a trade, are one of the primary devices traders use to minimize risk. It is important to know under what conditions you should use different types of stops—including protective stops, break-even stops and trailing stops. Moreover, you should be familiar with other types of mechanisms—such as good till cancel (GTC) orders—that you can use to lock in profits.

To maintain the discipline you need to adhere to your stops, you also may want to run historical simulations of the trading strategy you plan to use for specific stocks. Known as *back testing,* these simulations allow you to see how the set of conditions you have outlined for buying or selling a specific stock has worked in the past. These tests can heighten your level of discipline, because the more confident you are in your trading plan, the more likely you will be to see it all the way through.

From a psychological standpoint, to manage risk, you also have to know your comfort level for losses. You must ask yourself, for example, how you would react if you were facing a severe drawdown or were tagged with consecutive losses. In addition, you must ponder whether it is worth your while to spread your trading capital out across multiple stocks. By addressing these questions, you can figure out exactly how much cash you are willing to risk—both for a specific trade and over the course of a full trading day.

In this chapter we will take an in-depth look at all these important issues. Moreover, we will investigate the level of risk associated with tactics that are not used commonly, such as short selling. Extra caution may be needed when selling short because if you buy long, the stock suddenly shoots up, and you have not placed any stops, there is no limit to the amount you could lose.

Lastly, we will explore the risks associated with borrowing money to trade—or trading *on margin.* Many traders use margin to leverage their accounts, but if you are not careful, you could wind up on the wrong end of a margin call.

MINIMIZING LOSSES AND LOCKING IN PROFITS THROUGH STOPS

No matter what your trading style is, stop-loss orders can help you reduce your risk and boost profits. When you use stops, you can either input automatic stops via your direct access system or keep mental tabs of where you want to exit a trade and enter stops manually.

The automatic stop process calls for you to authorize your direct access system to make the trade for you at your preset stop level. For instance, if you buy a stock at 57⅛, you can instruct the system to automatically sell if the stock dips to 56. In contrast, when you are taking a mental approach, you have a stop-loss figure in your head—but it is then entirely up to you to exit that trade when the stock hits your stop loss.

While automated stops are a nice tool to have at your disposal, most traders feel more comfortable maintaining mental stops. By entering manual stops, these traders theorize, they can maintain total control over their orders and retain final decision-making power. And this can be important, especially if a trader decides at the last second that he or she wants to let a stock run a little or slide a bit.

Ken Johnson, sixthmarket.com's CEO, says that thanks in large part to stop-loss orders, minimizing risk is really "not so difficult." His approach is fairly simple: Prior to every trade, he sets his stop loss and sticks to it. If you take this approach, then, if you set your stop loss at, say, 1.5 points, then you know you are never going to lose more than that amount. "If I will only do those kinds of trades, my risk is taking care of itself, as long as I will execute to those [risk] parameters," says Johnson. "But you've got to understand, by looking at spreads and [seeing] how thinly traded the stock is, that when you tell yourself you're playing with 1.5 points, that is all you're playing for."

Essentially, there are three types of stop-loss orders: the protective stop, the break-even stop, and the trailing stop. The traditional *protective stop,* as the name implies, is intended to protect traders from incurring large losses. Usually, traders set their protective stop somewhere below the price at which they entered an issue. Smart traders will keep a mental record of their stop loss and, if and when their stock reaches that magic number, be disciplined enough to exit the trade without any hesitation. "If you buy at 42 and your stop is 41, get out if it hits 41. Don't think about it, don't agonize over it, don't worry about it," advises Johnson. "The truth is, if you're good at this, and you're seeing 10, 20, 40, 60, or 100 opportunities a day, you're not going to live with this one trade."

The *break-even stop,* meanwhile, is placed at the price level at which you entered a stock. If you jumped into a stock at 46¼, for example, then this is the price at which you would set your break-even stop. Sometimes traders employ a break-even stop after they have already cashed in part of a winning trade. Traders who do so can ensure that, at the very least, they will not lose any money on the rest of the shares they hold for that winning stock.

However, Howard Abell, cofounder of invest2know.com, says that just because you are on the winning end of a trade, you should not necessarily raise your stop to the break-even level. "There is nothing magic about break-even," he says. "If you buy a stock at 50 and your risk is 48, and the stock goes to 50½, does that mean you should bring [your stop] up to 50? I'm not sure about that."

In the aforementioned scenario, Abell says, you should take a second to reevaluate your position before moving your stop to break-even—unless your profit objective is 50½. "Then, you have a legitimate reason for . . . bringing the stop to break-even," he says.

On top of the break-even and protective stops, there is also the *trailing stop*. Traders typically use this type of stop when they are in the money and want to lock in some or all of their profits. Sometimes technical traders use trailing stops because no matter how good a stock looks on a chart, you can never really be sure how much it is going to move, says Johnson. Despite positive indications from your chart, the stock may not break through its resistance level. Moreover, the possibility exists that the stock could tumble quickly all the way back to your break-even or protective stop.

"If the stock moves 4 points my way, do I really want to let stock come all the way back down to my protective stop and lose all that profit? Maybe not," says Johnson. "You may want to set a trailing stop a point below the high [for the stock for that day]. Then, if a stock moves up 4 points but falls back 1 point, I'm out."

Unfortunately, when you are on the winning end of a trade, sometimes you can be lulled into a false sense of security. You may be thinking that you have money to burn because you have already made a tidy profit on that stock. And in turn, you may convince yourself that you do not need to set a trailing stop because the money that you have made was not really yours to begin with.

However, Abell says that successful traders condition their minds against this type of carefree attitude. "People tend to think I'm playing with somebody else's money, but really that's hard-earned money that you've built up into that position. And there's no reason to give it back," says Abell. "What you should believe in, with all your heart, is that any increase, any profits that you have [made] in a stock, . . . is your money."

Incorporating a trailing stop, says Abell, also can be challenging emotionally because at some point you are going to exit a profitable stock that continues to rise long after you decide to get out. At this point, of course, you may get distraught thinking about how much profit you left on the table. The thing to remember, though, is that although you bailed out early, you still made money on the trade. Moreover, if your risk-reward strategy is sound, many more money-making opportunities will come your way.

All in all, the trailing stop, when used intelligently, can increase a trader's success ratio. However, it is not the only mechanism traders use to lock in profits. A *good till cancel* (GTC) order is another device traders use to cash in on winning trades. A GTC is simply an order that is open to execution until it is canceled. Typically, a trader would enter a GTC immediately after he or she purchases a stock so that it could be sold automatically if it reaches his or her profit goal. For example, a trader could buy a stock at 52⅛ and place a GTC to sell that stock at 55. Then, if the stock ever hits 55, the GTC goes into effect, and your computer system attempts to sell the stock at that price.

However, even though there is a decent chance that you will get your desired fill if you enter a GTC and the stock hits your price, there is no guarantee. Nasdaq orders are filled based on price/time priority, so if your GTC is not near the top of the list of sell orders, you may not get your trade. "The amount of shares you want to trade have to be there, and you have to be in the list quick enough to get them. The stock may hit [your GTC price], but you may be far enough down the queue that . . . [the order] doesn't get executed," says Johnson.

One of the potential drawbacks of GTCs is that you could miss out on some heavy profits if the stock for which you placed a GTC goes on a bull run. Keeping this in mind, it is extremely important to carefully weigh the direction in which your stock is headed before you place a GTC.

Given the potential of GTCs to inhibit profit, some online trading experts are adamantly opposed to traders using them. Abell, a former principal of the proprietary trading firm Skylane Trading, describes the GTC as a lazy type of order that does not present many benefits to active short-term traders. In fact, he recommends that active traders avoid GTCs because they enhance the possibility for errors and create "bookkeeping headaches." Moreover, Abell says that active online traders do not need to enter GTCs because their job requires them to keep an extremely close eye on their open positions and stock portfolio—as well as on the overall state of the market.

GOING SHORT

Direct access traders have to be particularly vigilant about monitoring positions when they are on the short end of a trade. As we discussed at length in Chapter 3, *short selling* takes place when a trader borrows shares to sell a stock in anticipation of buying that stock back later at a cheaper price.

Short selling is riskier than the traditional stock trading method of "buy low, sell high," which is also known as *longing a stock*. If you go long, the absolute worst thing that could happen—albeit extremely unlikely—is for the stock to tumble down to zero. However, in theory, at least if you short a stock, there is no limit to the amount of money you could lose if that issue—for one reason or another—goes on a prolonged bull run.

The thing to remember is that you must, at some point, buy back the shares of the stock you originally borrowed. Thus, if, for example, you decided to short a stock at 36¼, and then, all of a sudden, that same stock suddenly shoots up to 50, you could be in trouble.

Of course, this scenario would unfold only if you either have no stop loss or are willing to let stocks slip way beyond the maximum risk you said you would incur before shorting a stock. Just like when you are buying long, when shorting, your risk factor is reduced if you set your stop and stick to it. However, since you are indeed facing an unlimited risk factor when shorting, it is so much more important that you do not let losing trades slide past your risk blockade.

Harvey Houtkin, chairman and chief executive officer of the Mont-vale, N.J.–based day trading firm All-Tech Investment Group, says that shorting is really no more dangerous than going long. The key to success, he says, is to maintain your rules of discipline. "As a professional trader, you're supposed to be employing discipline and control.. . . .[So] you should be able to acknowledge when you are wrong and throw in the towel. If you don't do it, it's because you're just not trading well," says Houtkin, whose firm also owns and operates the Attain electronic communication network (ECN). "Most people know exactly what they're supposed to do—they just don't do it because they don't want to take the loss or don't want the pain or don't want to feel that they're wrong."

While agreeing that it is important to be disciplined when you are engaged in shorting, Abell says that traders who short also should consider adjusting their risk-reward ratios so that they are taking only "very small losses." If you "maintain a methodology that stipulates you will only take small risks," he says, then short selling can be a "profitable adjunct to a successful" trading strategy.

Not surprisingly, your personal trading style also could have an impact on degree of risk you take on while shorting. One trader, speaking on condition of anonymity, says the level of risk for short sellers is directly related to the strategies they employ. This source says that a scalper who shorts a stock is taking on significantly less risk than a swing trader because the scalper is going to exit the trade much more quickly. "When I am shorting, which is rare, I will change my strategy. I will try to make more trades, with higher volumes, and with quicker turnover," he says. "In most situations, I think shorting isn't that much riskier. If you can recognize trends, and you want to scalp for small percentage points here and there, and you're going to use stop orders, it's no riskier than anything else—because you're going to be able to get in and out very quickly. But obviously, if you hold your positions a little bit longer, then it's a lot riskier, because then you increase the possibility of a greater swing."

Short selling, indeed, is not something that appeals to a lot of swing traders—particularly those who hold positions for multiple days. "Unless the entire market is in a down trend, I'm really never comfortable short selling," says Peter Sweeney, a full-time active day trader who uses swing trading as his primary strategy. "There's always the nagging thought in the back of your mind that you short sell a stock for 15 and then somebody comes in and buys it overnight for 38."

Omega Research's Ralph Cruz understands Sweeney's cautious approach to shorting. Noting that many stocks today are subject to "crazy valuations," he says that short selling is definitely riskier than going long. "If I invest $1000 in a stock and I buy it, the most that can happen is I lose $1000. But if I short it and it goes up 10 times, I've lost $10,000," Cruz explains.

These fears are shared by at least some traders in the direct access community. Johnson says that during a recent speech he gave at a trading convention in Las Vegas, only about 10 of 400 traders in the audience raised their hands when he asked how many people have ever executed a short sell. "People don't short sell. They don't understand it, and because they don't understand it, they're afraid of it—they just don't get it. And if you don't understand and you're afraid, then, yes, it's risky. But not if you understand it," says Johnson.

Mostly, he says, traders tend to shy away from shorting because they are afraid of the unknown. They are more cautious about shorting a stock because they have either never done it before or have not experienced success shorting. Ultimately, however, if you have intimate knowledge of how a stock trades on a Nasdaq level II screen, or if you know how to read stock charts, then shorting should not present any major difficulties—because you are as likely to recognize when a stock is going to tumble as when it is going to rise, says Johnson.

PROS AND CONS OF BACK TESTING

Beyond stop-loss orders, one other potential method for reducing risk is to perform a so-called back test of the strategy you plan to use to trade a specific stock. In simple terms, the *back test* is really a historical simulation that allows you to see how the set of conditions you have outlined for buying or selling a stock has worked in the past.

Cruz says that back testing can improve a trader's confidence and discipline because if he or she knows that a strategy has produced good results historically, he or she probably will stand by his or her original plan. "A lot of times, being successful is not [just about] having a plan, but being able to stick with it. So the more you understand historically how a strategy has behaved and performed, the more likely it is you are going to be able to stick with it . . . and the more confidence you're going to have in the approach itself," he says.

Like Cruz, Abell thinks that back testing can help a trader "ferret out" potentially robust strategies to use for specific stocks. However, he also asserts that until you have tested a strategy in "real time," you definitely cannot be sure that you are going to generate positive results with it. "Just because it's worked well in past doesn't guarantee you anything," says Abell.

As an alternative to back testing, he says, you could devise a strategy that you initially only jot down on paper. At the end of each trading day, you could then evaluate that strategy to see whether you could have entered and exited a stock at the price points you identified in the yet-to-be-used strategy you dreamed up.

However, Cruz says, it is important to see how a strategy has performed in the past for two main reasons: (1) to determine whether the strategy had made any money previously and (2) to figure out whether it has had severe drawdowns or has a record of lots of consecutive winners or losers.

Too often, says Cruz, when traders need some sage advice, they do not have an outlet to turn to. If you ask a "trading guru," he says, you will be told when exactly you should buy or sell specific stocks, but you will not be provided with any negative examples of how a strategy has performed in the past. "Unless you have the opportunity to back test your idea, it's hard to have a lot of confidence in what you're doing," says Cruz. "Of course, just because [a strategy has] worked in the past doesn't guarantee it's going to work in the future. But if it hasn't made a penny in the past, you . . . [can be] pretty sure you don't want to risk your money on this strategy."

Through a product dubbed TradeStation, Omega Research offers investors the ability to perform a back test of a strategy during the course of an actual trading day. Via TradeStation, says Cruz, a trader can test a "year of 1-minute bar charts" in only a minute or two. And if you do not have time to test your strategy during the day, you can run historical simulations either before the open or after the close.

Performing these back tests, Cruz adds, is also a lot cheaper way of gaining experience than making actual trades. "You can lose hundreds of thousands or millions of dollars in historical simulations and not have to worry about learning at your own expense," he says.

TRADING ON MARGIN

One tool that many direct access traders use to leverage their accounts is margin. When you trade *on margin,* you are essentially borrowing money from your brokerage firm to buy stocks. By doing so, traders increase their buying power. "The professional day trader is pushing his [or her] margin cnvelope as far as he [or she] can. . . . Assuming he [or she] is a good trader, he [or she] wants to be as leveraged in the market as he [or she] can," says Johnson.

Naturally, however, if you are going to borrow money to trade, you have to be more careful about protecting your equity than you would if you were trading strictly from your own capital base. In fact, risk management for margin traders is analogous to bookkeeping for accountants—one false step, and you might be looking for another line of work.

Moreover, in the future, traders using margin may have to pay even closer attention to risk. Today, equity traders are able to borrow money on a 2:1 basis. In late 1999, however, both the New York Stock Exchange (NYSE) and the National Association of Securities Dealers (NASD, Nasdaq's parent) announced proposals for new rules that would raise the margin basis to 4:1 for traders who make at least four intraday trades per week. Simultaneously, the proposal called for the minimum account balance for traders who use such a margin basis to increase from $2000 to $25,000.

At the time of this writing, these proposals still had not been given the green light by the Securities and Exchange Commission (SEC). However, if they eventually get approved, an active online trader trading NYSE or Nasdaq issues would be able to buy $300,000 worth of stock, for example, if he or she has $75,000 in his or her account. Today, of course, a trader with the same amount of money in his or her account could buy only a more modest $150,000 worth of stock.

The reason traders will have to be even more vigilant about risk if the margin basis is raised to 4:1 is that the money they are borrowing is simply a loan. Traders are responsible for any of the losses that take place with the borrowed money. For instance, if a trader has $100,000 in his or her account and grabs an additional $300,000 worth of margin, he or she must pay up if he or she loses any of that $300,000.

However, the good thing about margin—aside from the buying leverage it gives you—is that you only have to pay interest on the loan if you hold onto your positions overnight. Moreover, if you buy a stock on margin and then sell it within the same day, you are not going to be subject to a *margin call*—a process in which your broker requires you to put more money into your account as collateral against the money the broker loaned you.

Typically, a margin call occurs only when your account has taken a severe hit. The loss level at which you get cut off depends on each individual brokerage firm. However, if, for example, you were trading on margin and lost 75 percent of your original trading capital, then you definitely would be subject to a call.

Traders who hold positions after the close, says Houtkin, are the individuals you really have to watch closely when it comes to trading on margin However, if the new margin proposals get approved, the 4:1 borrowing level will apply only to traders who trade intraday. The margin basis will continue to be 2:1 for overnight trades. "I don't think margin is very dangerous if you know a . . . [person] is going to complete his [or her] trade the same day. . . . It's the person who takes home a position overnight—who takes home his [or her] 5000 shares of Nokia at 55 and then the stock opens up at 41. That's the . . . [person] who's in big trouble," says Houtkin.

This said, there is one type of call that direct access traders would have to deal with if they trade on an intraday basis. Known as a *technical call,* this call stipulates that a trader has to deposit money into his or her account if he or she buys more stock than the total amount of combined capital he or she has in the account. For example, says Houtkin, if a trader has $100,000 in his or her account and borrows money on a 2:1 basis, he or she cannot purchase more than $200,000 in stock during the course of the day. If, for instance, that trader bought $230,000 worth of stock, the brokerage firm would then send out a technical call that would require the trader to deposit an additional $15,000 into his or her account.

Taking all the facts noted above into consideration, one question remains: Do you have to significantly alter your risk strategy if you trade on margin? Well, that depends on whom you ask. Abell says that margin accounts should be used only by active online traders who slash their risk by taking very small losses.

"There's no such thing as waiting for the market to come back when you are on margin," he says. "No matter how much you believe in its upside potential, if a stock has violated your risk parameters, you get out and wait for another opportunity." Like Houtkin, Abell says that the traders who assume the most risk while trading on margin are those who hold positions after the close—particularly when the market goes into a tailspin.

Similarly, Johnson says that as long as they are not carrying home losing positions overnight, traders should use margins—especially the 2:1 margin—to leverage their buying power. However, he also says that smart traders should make sure that the "math" is in their favor when they are borrowing money. One way to do this, says Johnson, is to make "high-probability trades with good risk-return ratios."

Still, despite his suggestion that margin traders should be more selective about the types of stocks they trade, Johnson asserts that traders who borrow money to trade on a daily basis are not taking on that much more risk than traders who use only their own capital to trade. From 1998 to 1999, Johnson served as the president of Cornerstone Securities, one of the largest day trading shops in the United States. And in 1999, 550 day traders at Cornerstone performed 250 million trades—but none of them ever got into any margin trouble, claims Johnson.

Meanwhile, while conceding that margin can spell trouble for traders who misuse it, Cruz describes margin as a tool of "convenience" that can help you build your account and manage your assets more effectively. Unfortunately, he says, some traders who lose their shirts unjustly blame margin for their demise. "Traders who are going to trade what they can't afford to lose . . . are going to tend to do it with or without margin," Cruz asserts.

Unlike some of his colleagues, Houtkin believes that margin is totally unrelated to the trader's level of risk. What's more, Houtkin says that since a "true" day trader cuts his or her losses, active trading is, to "a certain extent," less risky than long-term investing. "On balance, a day trader is much more hands on. But there are a lot of day traders who really don't day trade. They go ahead and become investors, and they lose a lot of money because they buy stock and don't take [their] losses," says Houtkin.

Since he believes margin traders are not assuming any greater risk than anyone else, Houtkin would like to see the whole process of increasing the margin ratio speeded up. The exchanges, he says, have been tossing this idea around for "a couple of years" but have not been in a hurry to implement it.

The limits of today's margin conceivably could force a trader to go outside his or her broker to borrow money. And if you are in need of money and have "maxed out" your margin, one other way to quickly and simply acquire the equity you need is through a practice known as *journaling*. Journaling occurs when one trader at a day trading shop agrees to transfer funds electronically to another trader.

The process, explains Houtkin, only requires the trader supplying the money to fill out a single form. That trader, he says, is not required to cut a check and is not subject to any waiver fees or charges. "People do it among themselves as a courtesy to one another. It's like a revolving credit line in between the traders. They help each other out," says Houtkin. Since the money's "already in house," he says, it often takes just a day for the trader supplying the loan to get his or her money back.

Recently, journaling has come under scrutiny by some sources who have criticized the practice in the media. A few stock market participants have even claimed that these loans only enable traders with inadequate equity to continue trading. Houtkin contends, however, that a day trading firm denying the request of one of its traders to journal $10,000 to another trader is akin to a bank refusing a client's request to transfer money from his or her account to the account of another of the bank's clients. ". . . [Journaling] is perfectly legal. There's nothing morally or legally wrong with it," he says. "It's your money, . . . [so you should be able to] do what you want with it."

RISK-REWARD RATIO, RISK EXPOSURE, AND OTHER FACTORS

Margin is just one of many elements that you have to consider to calculate your *risk-reward ratio*—a ratio that weighs the amount you are willing to lose versus the profit you hope to gain. On the way to establishing your risk-reward ratio, you must take into account not only your margin level but also the average number of shares you plan to trade—a practice that is also known as *sizing your position.*

To size your position for each individual stock you trade, you should consider your capital, the number of points you are going to risk, and the percentage of winning trades you make. Collectively, these facts not only will enable you to determine your share size but also will keep you abreast of the capital you need to continue to trade.

For instance, according to one popular mathematical risk formula, if you have $100,000 in capital, your risk is 1.5 points, and your trades are successful 55 percent of the time, you must hold onto roughly 40 percent of your total equity to remain in business. However, Johnson says that regardless of any formulas that you use, you can develop a successful risk-reward ratio if you follow two simple guidelines: "Don't second guess yourself at the stop loss, and don't get greedy at the exit."

All this being said, when calculating your risk, there are two other important factors to consider: a stock's volatility and the price range. Obviously, more volatile stocks are going to have wider daily price ranges, and accordingly, you are going to have to assume a higher level of risk. In contrast, less volatile stocks are going to have narrower daily ranges. Either way, you have to factor volatility and range into your risk-reward ratio. "If something looks like it's poised for a move but you know that its daily range is only a buck, then you shouldn't be risking a whole dollar," says Sweeney.

In terms of managing your risk exposure, Sweeney adds, it is important for you to have the capability to look at your gains and losses "arbitrarily" at any given time. And it is easier to accomplish this, he says, if you evaluate your real-time profit and loss (P&L) figures based on points rather than dollar amounts. "When I start thinking about dollars, I have too much at risk. You get shaken out of positions, and you [tend to] cut your winners off because every tick means too many dollars," says Sweeney.

Diversification—or spreading out your equity across multiple stocks—is one other way to potentially ameliorate risk. Cruz, for one, believes in the concept of minimizing risk through diversification. "You may be getting killed on one security, but you may be offsetting that with the success you are having someplace else," he says.

However, keeping track of multiple open positions is much easier said than done—especially if you are a momentum trader or a scalper. In fact, if you are typically in and out of a trade in seconds or minutes, you may be increasing your risk by dabbling in more than two or three stocks at a time.

Sweeney says that your level of diversification should be directly proportional to the number of different stocks you can focus on simultaneously. "It depends on how many charts you can watch or how many level II screens you can watch at the same time. I find it virtually impossible to look at more than three," he says.

SCALPING VERSUS SWING TRADING

On top of the factors we have already mentioned, your specific level of risk is also contingent on the type of trading in which you engage. Traders who practice swing trading, for example, face a high risk factor because they may be holding a stock anywhere from 2 to 5 days—a period of time in which a stock could fluctuate significantly. "That approach is the one that can have the biggest gains. But it's also a riskier strategy . . . [because] you can have a stock run 3 or 4 points and then fall back past your entry point," says Johnson.

It takes a person with above-average discipline and mental toughness, he adds, to tolerate the up-and-down high-risk nature of swing trading. However, Omega's Cruz says that it is not necessarily true that scalping is inherently less risky than swing trading. "If you have a good approach and good foundation, you're in good shape. I'd rather have a good swing trading strategy than a bad scalping strategy," he says.

Cruz adds that he is very skeptical of scalping, because you are aiming for relatively tiny gains, and "one bad move can really wipe out a whole day's profit." Scalpers, he says, can manage their risk successfully if they have a style that works consistently. However, Cruz also wonders aloud whether it is worth the dedication and time it takes for a scalper to snag an eighth here and a quarter there. "It's a question of cost benefit," he says.

Whether you choose to engage in a high- or low-risk strategy depends, at least in part, on your mental makeup. A strategy that has proven successful for one trader, says Cruz, may prove to be a disaster for another—possibly because he or she could not get through periods of severe drawdowns or wild swings in the market. This is why you must ask yourself, for example, how comfortable you would feel with a $2000 loss—or with three consecutive $1000 losses. The answers to these types of questions, says Cruz, should aid you in determining the average amount of money you are willing to risk per trade.

Obviously, there are a number of different things you can do to minimize risk. But perhaps the most sage—and yet simple—advice comes from Abell. Active online trading, he says, is a "process" that is based on the concept that the "smallest and first loss" is the best loss. "It has nothing to do with any individual trade," says Abell. "Therefore, the concept of taking very small losses and moving on to the next opportunity will stand you in good stead."

6

CASE STUDIES

To achieve success as a direct access trader, you have to be flexible. Since the stock market is in a continuous state of flux, you must be able to adjust your strategy accordingly. Moreover, you have to attain the knowledge and skills necessary to read and dissect a Nasdaq level II screen.

Along the way, you will have to find answers to several important questions, including: What are the key elements of my trading plan? Does my style mesh better with traditional trading or short selling? What are my profit and loss parameters? What are my execution options? What type of activity should I be looking for on level II? And what factors should I consider when I am concocting my risk-management plan?

Of course, it would be nearly impossible to understand the thought process that goes into active online trading without spending some one-on-one time with actual traders. Therefore, in this chapter we will crawl inside the minds of seven direct access traders.

Equipped with sophisticated trading software, these traders arrived at their current careers through varied backgrounds. However, from the airline pilot to the former stockbroker to the speech pathologist turned momentum trader, they all have two things in common: a strong desire to learn and a willingness to share their expertise and experiences with the rest of the investing public.

DON MERZ: SAY HELLO TO MR. CONFIDENCE

For most of us, simultaneously monitoring and analyzing several fast-moving stocks is a difficult—if not downright impossible—task. For 32-year-old direct access trader Don Merz, however, it is second nature. "The one thing in the whole world I've been good at is this. I'll take on any market maker, any trader, anyone on any day. I have no problem with that. I'm not trying to be cocky, but I know I'm good at this—really good at it," he says.

At first glance, of course, such brash talk may seem like gratuitous self-promotion. However, if you believe that success breeds confidence, then Merz's ultraconfident frame of mind is neither unwarranted nor surprising. After all, in 1999, he raked in more than $100,000 in profit. And from January to July 2000, Merz claims that he was in the black by roughly $750,000.

In other words, Merz may talk the talk, but he also walks the walk. Typically, he makes between 200 and 250 trades a day, with an average order size of 8000 shares. Moreover, throughout the course of a normal trading day, Merz often has eight different level II stock windows running at the same time. "If I could have 16 [stocks], I'd have 16 on here. There's just not enough room on the monitor," he says.

Merz describes himself as a scalper/momentum/swing trader "all wrapped up in one." But frankly, he says, he cares for none of these tags—especially with the way day traders have been portrayed by the mainstream media. "If somebody wants to label me a scalp trader or they want to label me a day trader, you can label me whatever you want. I'm making seven figures a year. Do you think I really care what people call me? What are the people making that are saying this stuff? . . . Call me whatever you want, I don't care," Merz says defiantly.

Fueled by his experience, desire, and knowledge of the stock industry, Merz has made up to $47,000 in single day. Moreover, during a recent

12-month stretch, he had several days where he raked in between "$20,000 and $30,000," he says. However, while Merz is now enjoying the fruits of his labor, success certainly has not come overnight. Indeed, starting back in the late 1980s, Merz took a circuitous route to his current career.

After attending college for a couple of years, Merz, who majored in business and finance, decided to take "a little sabbatical" to see if he could make his mark in the financial services world. Coincidentally, at that time, he was dating a woman whose father worked as the head trader at the securities firm Credit Suisse First Boston. And following a few visits to the head trader's office, Merz's interest in trading stocks gained momentum, and he decided that he would like to try his hand as a stockbroker.

Subsequently, Merz went out and grabbed his series 7 broker's license. After a short stint as a stockbroker, however, he realized that job was not for him. "Doing cold calling and being a stockbroker and all that stuff, it wasn't me. Whoever would . . . [lie] the best was . . . [the best] stockbroker. They didn't care about what happened to other people's money. . . . They just cared what happened in their pocket," he recalls.

As luck would have it, in "late 1994 or early 1995," Merz started dating a different woman, whose uncle owned a trading firm on Long Island. During his tenure at that firm, he learned the ins and outs of Nasdaq level II, using momentum trading techniques to make money for his clients.

Eventually, says Merz, he moved on to take a position with a "Wall Street firm," where he was "trading on behalf of the firm and handling orders for other people." But over the course of time, he grew tired of working his tail off to generate profits for other people. "I said, 'Why am I making money for everybody else, and I'm getting [just] a little payoff?' It didn't make sense. So I said, 'You know what, that's it. I'm going to start making money for myself.' "

Armed with this new attitude, in 1998 Merz began trading for himself, as a full-fledged direct access trader. For about a year or so, Merz bounced around a couple of different day trading shops before finally ending up at his current place of business—Millennium Brokerage.

When he shows up to trade each day at Millennium's Woodcliff Lake, New Jersey–based office, Merz feels that he has an edge over many of the people he is going to be competing with—thanks in part to his experience on the professional trading side of the business. From a technology perspective, he says, he has got a leg up because he began using direct access systems all the way back in 1997 and now knows just about every system (including his incumbent platform from Tradecast) "backwards and forwards." From a business perspective, Merz adds, he is a step ahead because he knows what it is like to trade orders on behalf of clients. "I know everything about the market makers. I know what they do and how they handle their orders. I know that side, and I know the individual investor side. So that gives me a big advantage," he says.

Style Points

Usually Merz trades stocks priced at $20 and under. Occasionally, however, he will enter orders for stocks in the $30 to $50 range. However, in order to reach out for these more expensive stocks, Merz says, he needs to see some data that indicate that a stock is about to make a run or break out of its range.

Noting that he makes $40,000 on some days and $1000 on others, Merz says that it is difficult for him to attach a dollar figure to his average daily profit. Similarly, he says that while his average order size is 8000 shares, the size can fluctuate anywhere from 4000 to 16,000 shares, depending on the day.

On a daily basis, however, he does consider several factors before entering an order. The very first thing that catches Merz's eye is a stock's volume. At a minimum, Merz says, a stock needs to have a volume of 100,000 shares for him to even consider trading it. "Volume precedes price movement, so you have to have the volume," he says.

On top of looking at volume, Merz eyes charts, scans the wire to see if there is any breaking news on the stock, and records a mental note of the specific market participants on the bid side and the offer side. His interest in a security really peaks, he says, if any market maker or electronic communication network (ECN) starts "bidding the stock up" at the open. "If you've got a stock that closes at six [the previous day], and it's been bid up to six-and-a-half, seven dollars, or whatever, [then you know] there's something going on," says Merz.

To measure a stock's relative strength, Merz also sometimes checks to see how a stock is doing in relation to other stocks in its industry grouping. "If I'm buying a semiconductor stock, I've got to look at [similar] stocks, [and ask] 'How's the stock doing in comparison to others in its sector?' " he says.

For the most part, Merz uses his charting and volume data to trade stock intraday, based on the market's momentum. But every so often, he says, he will use a swing trading strategy to take a trade home overnight. "There are some stocks that I buy during the day, and they come up a little bit and they look great on the chart. And I'll hold them because they look great on the chart," says Merz.

Moreover, Merz also, on occasion, will hold stocks that are the beneficiary of positive end-of-day news. "A lot of times after hours [those stocks will] gap up or [someone will] gap them up in the morning," he explains.

Getting Executed

From a routing standpoint, the exact destination to which Merz sends an order for any given stock depends largely on who is on the offer and who is on the bid in that stock. "A lot of times I'll go out and I'll just take out the whole offer if I like the stock. If I wanted to buy, I'd go in for the whole thing," he says.

Five to ten percent of the time, Merz routes his orders through the Small Order Execution System (SOES). The rest of the time, he reaches his final execution destination via either SelectNet Preference or direct connectivity to ECNs.

Merz says that he only uses SOES if he cannot get an order executed through SelectNet Preference. Too often, he says, when you preference a market maker via SelectNet, he or she will wait far too long to respond to your order, and the price of the stock you want to buy will begin to run up. In such instances, Merz sometimes reroutes that order through SOES.

"Market makers have got their orders, but they're watching 30 stocks. They're watching 30 stocks, and all they have is one level II screen in front of them. They're working the orders. And I guess they don't see [some orders] or whatever," Merz explains. "So now you're sitting there and . . . you say, 'Hey, you know what, I'm not getting done on SelectNet, so let me go in via a different . . . [routing system] to get the stock.' "

One other alternative Merz could tap into is SelectNet Broadcast, but he says that he completely shuns this version of SelectNet because he does not want his order displayed to the entire market making community. "I won't go out and use Broadcast because what's the sense? Nobody wants to touch you on a SelectNet Broadcast [order] . . . because that's when everybody sees it," says Merz.

Although he is aware of SelectNet's 10-second no-cancellation rule, he says that he is not bothered by it because he only uses SelectNet when he "really wants a stock." Like most other direct access traders, Merz would prefer to send an order directly to an ECN. Unfortunately, however, ECNs are sometimes nowhere to be found on the offer side of a stock. In such situations, Merz is forced to go through SelectNet because it is the only way he can reach the market makers who are offering a stock at the price he wants. "Most of the time there are ECNs [on the offer], but [sometimes] there's no ECNs, just market makers. And the only way to get it through them is to preference [them through] SelectNet, because if you [go] through SOES, you only can get up to 1000 shares [filled]," says Merz.

In the premarket, however, ECNs represent the only choice for direct access traders who want to execute trades. If you want to grab a stock prior to the opening, says Merz, you have to route an order to an ECN— because market makers are not obligated to fill your order. "You've got to investigate stocks that have jumped up from their high from the day before. If a stock zapped up a point, you got to find out why, . . . and the only way you find out is by looking at the level of ECN interest in the stock," he says. "From 9 to 9:30, you can route an order to a specific ECN, through SelectNet, and get [it] filled. . . . Market makers, on the other hand, are under no obligation to fill [your order] before 9:30 A.M."

Mental Discipline

Despite the fact that he does not believe stop-loss orders are as effective now as they once were, Merz says that traders need to maintain mental stops. Like the majority of his direct access brethren, Merz prefers a mental stop over an automatic stop—primarily because it gives him the power to change his stop level in accordance with how a specific stock is performing during the course of the day.

Too often, he says, he has seen traders get burned using automatic stops—because they are forced to exit a trade too soon. "Their stock hits the stop loss, the machine executes the trade for them, and then, all of the sudden, the stock rebounds and shoots right back up," Merz explains.

The mental stop, on the other hand, gives direct access traders the power to "evaluate the market" and decide whether they want to let the stock run "another eighth or a quarter" after it hits their stop level, says Merz. "With mental stop loss, I get to handle the order myself—I don't relinquish control of the order," he says. "If I let the machine handle it, I don't know how . . . the order is going to get executed or what device it's going to get routed through. [For example], is it going to go out via SelectNet or it is getting sent straight to an ECN?"

Prior to 1997, Merz says, it made more sense to adhere to a strict stop loss because, at that time, you could get rid of the full amount of shares you wanted to sell at the price you wanted. "Back then, when . . . [market makers were required to display] 1000 shares, more people were doing momentum because the markets were moving a little differently and people were SOESing [each other], and [then] you were actually getting the 1000 shares and knocking the guy out of the box," Merz recalls.

However, Merz says that today, stop-loss orders are less effective because market makers on a trader's level II display are "showing no size." Moreover, he notes that per SOES rules, if a market maker fills an order for, say, 100 shares, then that market maker has the right to wait another 17 seconds before filling another order at that same price. Such a delay, says Merz, really empowers market makers to cut off momentum in a stock. "The market makers are sitting there, and they're just fishing. They're looking for orders, too. They're looking for something to happen," he says.

Pointing to a stock on one of his level II windows that's filled with 100-share bids and offers from market makers, Merz says that it is sometimes very difficult to exit a position after you have purchased a stock. This is why today, if he does not see the size he wants on level II, Merz's inclination is to let a stock run a little after it hits his mental stop. "If the market makers are showing 100 shares each, and [I'm] sitting there with 8000 shares, what am I going to do, sit there and try to sell 100 shares at a time at each [different price] level? . . . Then I'd drive the price down myself," he says. "I'd rather ride it out. If the rest of the chart looks good [for the stock], I'll ride it out."

Risk Tips

The mental stop loss, of course, is one effective mechanism traders use to minimize risk. However, Merz says that keeping a mental stop is just one of a handful of ways you can reduce risk. The first thing one should do when evaluating a trade's risk, he says, is to make sure that your potential reward is greater than your potential risk. "When you even buy a stock, you don't want to risk more than you're going to [get in] reward. . . . [I'm not] going to risk losing a couple of thousand dollars to make $125," Merz says.

Unfortunately, he says, traders sometimes create their own risk problems by getting too attached to the stocks they are trading. And when that happens, they have problems getting out of a position. "I've seen some people buy a couple thousand shares of a stock at 14. And then it goes all the way down to $2, and they've still got the thing. Why? There is no reason for it," says Merz. "Stocks don't just go straight down. Unless it has got some bad news or something like that, [a stock] usually comes down gradually. . . . [So] if a stock goes through your stop loss, you've got to just get out. Don't get emotional over it. And don't think that just because you own a stock, it's going to go up."

For new direct access traders, he says, the best way to avoid getting too emotional about a string of consecutive losses is to take a break from trading. "When you lose like that, you're going to be trading on pure emotions, and you're going to be trading out of desperation. And if you trade out of desperation, you're doomed . . . [because] you're actually looking for something that's not there," he says. " So the best thing [for you to do] is get away from your machine, regroup and think about what you did, what happened [and] why it happened."

This advice notwithstanding, Merz says that, in all likelihood, he personally would not reduce his share size or take a break from trading if he were in the hole for, say, $10,000 an hour after the market opened. "I've had days when I walked in, and in the first half hour I'm down $10,000 or $15,000. But then I come back, and at the end of the day, I'm up $20,000. So what I do [to regroup from consecutive losses] is not [necessarily] what somebody else should do," he says. "It's all relative to how much you have and how long you've been doing it. . . . [But] I know I can sit down and make $10,000," says Merz.

One strategy Merz uses to take home profits—and minimize his risk—is *scaling out* of winning positions. Basically, this strategy calls for him to sell a portion of his shares if a winning stock he is holding reaches new heights. For example, if he is holding 8000 shares and he sees that the stock has broken past its resistance level or has achieved a new 52-week high, he might sell 4000 shares of that position to secure some profits. "Especially if the stock is moving up and it's got a great trend in the chart. . . . I'll lock in some of the profits and let the rest run," says Merz.

Aside from locking in profits on winning positions, you also can attempt to reduce your risk by spreading out your trading capital across multiple stocks. However, this approach does not work for everybody.

While asserting that the multiple-position strategy could work well for upper-echelon direct access traders, Merz advises less experienced traders to steer clear of this strategy. "Starting out, if you've not been doing it too long, I wouldn't . . . [trade] more than two or three stocks at one time," he says. "[But] everything boils down to your experience in the market."

In Merz's case, experience even can pay big dividends when he is investing in his long-term account. For example, he says, early in the year 2000 he got a feeling that he should get rid of his long-term positions—even though stocks in his long-term portfolio were performing well at the time. The market, he noticed, had taken a slight dip in January, and he was not buying into the argument that it was going to bounce back quickly. "I don't know if it was dumb luck or just a gut feeling I had, . . . but I sold all my positions, everything. When that whole whack in the market came down, I was basically sitting on all cash. It was just, maybe, experience. I have experience in the market. . . . When everybody's panicking, that's when I started buying in again. It worked out great," he recalls.

Of course, if you are holding stocks overnight and you do panic, you could get yourself in some very serious trouble—especially if you are borrowing money to trade (also known as *trading on margin*). Currently, individual investors can only borrow money to trade on a 2:1 basis, but as we discussed earlier in this book, the SEC is evaluating proposals to boost that ratio to 4:1.

Still, Merz says that regardless of the amount you are borrowing, the only time trading on margin can really get you in trouble is if you are holding stocks overnight. "You're still risking your own money," he says "All . . . [margin is] doing is basically giving you a little more buying power. It's not like you're sitting here going okay, I've got $100,000 in the account, I've got $200,000 of buying power, let me buy $200,000 in stock and hold it. You know what I mean? Day trading is different. If I get a margin call, which hardly ever happens, I just meet it. Meet it, and that's it."

Selling Short and Holding Overnight
Traditionally, short selling and holding stocks overnight have been seen as two of the riskier strategies direct access traders could employ. From Merz's perspective, maintaining positions after the close is not any more dangerous than trading intraday—but selling short is. "I don't like to short

stocks. When you short a stock, you've got an unlimited downside. . . . I guess it's just a psychological thing for me," says Merz.

He says that part of the problem with short selling—which requires a trader to first sell a stock and then buy it back at a later date—is the SEC's uptick rule. This rule states that you have to wait for a stock to generate an uptick before you can short that stock. "I've got to worry about the stock going up before I can short, . . . [and] I'm not going to say 'Oh, the stock's going up. Let me short it and hold it for a couple of days, and hopefully it will come back down,' " Merz explains.

However, unless you are holding stocks for "the wrong reasons," keeping positions overnight—in contrast to short selling—is no more risky than day trading, says Merz. "If you're holding stocks just because they're down against you and you're not going to sell them, and you take the position for all the wrong reasons, yeah, that's wrong. But if you're buying it and saying okay, you know what . . . I'm going to stick with it . . . [because] it looks great on the chart, that's fine," he says.

You must trust your charts, says Merz, even if a stock has not performed well recently, and the market is about to come to a close. "Any reason that I can look at the chart and the chart's saying to . . . [me], 'Hey listen, this stock's going to go up,' [is a good reason to hold]," he says. "Not that it's guaranteed [to turn a profit], obviously, but unless some bad news or bad earnings are released, . . . you [should be] saying, 'Hey, this chart looks good; the stock just broke out of a range, [so] I'm going to hold it for a day or two and see what it does.' "

The trick, he says, is to get rid of the stock as soon as its starts looking bad on your charts. "Sometimes I'll turn around and the charts look great. And then, all of a sudden, they look horrible. At that point . . . that's it, I'm out," he says.

Stock Selection and Screen Features
When it comes to picking stocks to trade, Merz says he simply goes with "whatever's hot that day." For a period of time recently, he says, the hot stocks were in the business-to-business (B2B) sector, but the pharmaceuticals caught fire, and shortly thereafter, dot-com stocks were the stocks to trade. "I'm not going to sit there and play tech stocks when all the biotechs are hot. I'm not going to sit there and try to buy the biotechs if all the Internet [stocks] are hot. I go with whatever's going at the time," explains Merz.

Identifying healthy stock sectors, he says, can prove particularly important on days when the market is tanking. On those bearish days, there are fewer opportunities for traditional buy-low, sell-high traders to trade. During those times, however, you can still find opportunities if you can pinpoint one hot stock sector.

Merz says that industry trade shows, at which companies often launch new products, are one type of event that can spark a run in a specific stock sector. For instance, when the most recent PC (personal computer) Expo was held, technology stocks began to shoot up rapidly. "The . . . [tech companies] were showing their products at the conference, and everybody was getting hot on the ideas," Merz explains.

You have to be careful, however, because just as quickly as a sector can rise upward, it can come plummeting back down to earth. Nevertheless, Merz can at least take comfort in the fact that if he wants to find a stock to trade, he has got a lot of tools at his disposal.

On the top of Merz's trading screen there are three charts that track stocks according to various intraday time intervals. Beneath these charts sits a scrolling ticker that provides real-time data on all of Merz's open positions. Next to the ticker there is a pair of high/low boxes that report intraday highs and lows for specific stocks in which he is interested (one is for stocks priced $20 and below, and the other is for stocks price $30 and above). What's more, there is also a chart that tracks all the different stock indices (including the Dow Jones Industrial Average, the Nasdaq Composite, and the Standard & Poor's 500 futures) and a profit and loss box. "But I have days where I make $30,000 or $40,000, so, though I have a real-time P&L, I don't watch it all the time," Merz says.

Toward the bottom of his screen there are eight Nasdaq level II boxes displaying real-time data on eight different stocks. And the time and sales report for each stock is displayed right next to each of the level II windows.

Nasdaq's time and sales data have value, says Merz, but often are useless at the open. "Nasdaq's got to get . . . [its stuff] together. . . . Nasdaq's time and sales . . . [window is] so far behind . . . in the morning you can't tell what's going on sometimes—especially [during] a very active morning," Merz laments. "[Nasdaq] . . . should take money from this . . . [corporate restructuring it's] doing and put it over into . . . [its] systems."

However, he acknowledges that apart from the open, the time and sales window is important. If the time and sales data are up to speed,

Merz says, they can help you uncover the identity of a market maker who is driving the run of a specific stock. "Sometimes what market makers do is they'll take . . . [a stock] down, keep taking it down, taking it down, . . . [and] then, all of a sudden, you'll see a big [time and sales] print for a couple of hundred thousand shares go up, and, boom, he [or she] is gone from the offer. The stock's going up," he says. "A lot of times they'll take [a stock] down like that, and it will pop right up right after . . . they clean out the seller."

Via a pair of separate trading screens, Merz also can tap into a real-time news service provided by Wall Street Source (WSS) and monitor a day trader chat room. When he arrives at his office in the morning, Merz checks his WSS screen to see if there is any breaking news on any of the stocks he trades. Throughout the course of the day, meanwhile, Merz also glances up at his chat room monitor, hoping to get stock insights from one of the "700 pairs of eyes" that are contributing information to that site.

Through WSS, Merz says, he can find "market open news, trading news," and corporate data—as well as rumors and news on stock upgrades and downgrades. Via the chat room, on the other hand, Merz often gets tips about a stock that has reached a new 52-week high or broken through its resistance or support level.

Generally speaking, he says, people use the chat room to point out trends. However, Merz cautions that you should "never try to piggy-back" on the advice of other day traders without first checking out your own data. "You don't know their motives. So if somebody says a stock is about to break out, look at your own charts for that stock," he says.

Parting Thoughts

By the time his trading day ends, Merz, says, he is usually "wiped out." Typically, after the close of the market, he goes home, has dinner, relaxes, and on occasion, enjoys a swim. Regardless of whether he has a good day or a bad day, however, he does not take his work home with him.

Just as he tries to keep from getting too high or low during the course of his trading day, he tries to not get overly joyous or melancholy about his performance after the day is over. "This here is separate [from the rest of my life]," he says. "You have your ups and downs . . . [during] the day, . . . [but] I sleep well at night."

However, Merz does get emotional when he sees media reports that equate day trading with gambling—an analogy he describes as a "disgusting generalization." "I've been doing this for a long time. If I want to go roll the dice down in Vegas, fine, that's gambling. . . . [But] I'm taking calculated risks. I'm looking at all different kinds of charts and analysis," he says. "It's like any business. You've got to know your competition, and you've got to know what's going on."

Too many of the critics who are making the gambling analogy, Merz adds, have no clue how the stock market operates. "People just don't realize what's going on in the markets," he says. "They'll say stuff . . . [like] market makers are manipulating the stock. But market makers can't manipulate the stock . . . [because] they have to trade their order flows," he says.

The trader and the market, he says, are analogous to the fisher and the sea. Just as the fisher has to respect the sea, the trader has to respect the volatile nature of the market. However, Merz says that just as some fishers have been swallowed up by the sea, some traders have been "wiped out" by the market. "[The market] . . . is much bigger than you. Much, much bigger than you. You've got to ride the wave and ride along with it. Just go with it. You fight the market, and it will destroy you," Merz cautions. " Some people think [that] I'm going to make a fortune [quickly]. But the market will kick your . . . [butt] every time. It really will."

In order to defend against getting one's butt kicked, Merz says that it is absolutely imperative for an active online trader to use direct access technology. When you are using a direct access system, Merz says, you have "total control over the order." In contrast, he says, when you send a market order through an online discount broker, there is a decent chance that your order will not get a fill for a couple of minutes. And by that time, says Merz, the stock already may have "run up 2 or 3 points," and you may be "down a couple of thousand" dollars.

"It makes no sense to me to even try trading like that," he concludes. "To do what we do for trading, you really need to have a direct access real-time system. As soon as I put out the order, if I'm executed, I'm done. I know it instantly. There's no ifs, ands, or buts about it."

CHRIS CROPLEY: YOUNG GUN SETS SIGHTS ON DIRECT ACCESS MASTERY

When 23-year-old Chris Cropley sets out to make his living each day, he wants to be consumed by his job. Indeed, in his own words, he "needs" to be "sweating bullets" to thrive in his daily work environment. Thus it should come as no big surprise that Cropley is now attempting to make his mark in the anxiety-ridden, pressure-packed realm of direct access trading.

Trying to make a living as a short-term online trader can be a daunting task. However, Cropley, an Alaska native who recently graduated from a technology program run by Devry Institutes in Kansas City, Missouri, is no stranger to challenges. After he graduated from Devry, the ambitious Cropley founded a computer networking firm dubbed Cropley.com.

Although he still runs his networking firm, Cropley got the itch to try something new shortly after launching his dot-com. He needed a new challenge. And then Cropley witnessed a friend of his execute stock trades via Real Tick III, a direct access system. "After I saw . . . [Real Tick], I thought, 'Ooh, how cool is that,' " he says. At that time, the seeds for Cropley's entrance into the direct access trading realm were planted.

Prior to getting a glimpse of Real Tick III, however, Cropley had executed a few trades with a traditional broker. Subsequently, he transitioned his money into an account with Ameritrade. However, after seeing how difficult it was just to execute a limit order through the online discount broker, Cropley quit Ameritrade.

Then, in December 1999—fueled by capital he raised through his networking firm—Cropley set up an online account with the direct access broker CyBerCorp. To get up to speed on the ins and outs of direct access trading, Cropley initially read books on the subject and talked with friends who use similar software packages. Like most new direct access traders, however, Cropley hit some rough patches in his first few months on the job.

Without divulging specific dollar figures, Cropley says that within his first 3 months of direct access trading, he lost 50 percent of the money he had in his initial CyBerCorp account (this loss, in fact, forced him to "recapitalize"). However, from March to August 2000, he increased his trading capital by 120 percent, giving him a net gain of 70 percent during his first 8 months of direct access trading.

For Cropley, the climb out of the red and into the black actually began back in February, when he started to make use of a trading system tailored to his individual style. At that time, one of the things he decided was to set maximum daily profit and risk levels. "If I make over $5000, I'm done for the day, . . . [and] if I lose three trades, I'm done for the day," says Cropley.

The maximum loss Cropley is willing to absorb on any single trade is $250, and he expects to make an average profit of between $500 and $1000 (per trade). Coincidentally, Cropley's average share size is between 500 and 1000.

One of the most important components of his overall trading plan is the entry point. For each individual stock he is monitoring, Cropley— who executes between 12 and 24 trades a day—knows the exact price level at which he wants to enter a buy or short order.

When Cropley is thinking about entering a position, he analyzes charts to get a read on a stock's momentum and figure out whether the stock has been overbought or oversold. On a daily basis, he has four charts that he consistently takes a peak at: the 1-minute, 1-day, 5-minute, and 5-day charts.

Integrated with these charts are "five or six indicators," including "Bollinger bands and stochastics," says Cropley. Through patterns these indicators form on the charts, Cropley gets a good read on how a stock has behaved in the past.

On top of gazing at his short-term charts, Cropley also occasionally glances at a 365-day stock chart. "A lot of times you'll look at something and say 'Oh my gosh, this thing is on fire,' and then you'll look back 6 months and see that the stock is trying to catch up to where it was 6 months ago," he says.

However, while he has a solid idea about where he is going to enter a position, Cropley says that he does not identify a specific exit point prior to making a trade. "I leave . . . [the exit point] pretty shallow," he says.

Feel-Good Philosophy

The measure of success Cropley has achieved as a direct access trader can be at least partly attributed to his state of mind. Going into each day, he will only trade if he feels physically and mentally stable. "If I was out late partying last night . . . , then I probably won't trade. Or if I had a bad day and am not feeling 100 percent, I won't trade. . . . It's not worth it," says Cropley.

When he's functioning properly, Cropley will wake up early in the morning and turn on CNBC to see if the market has chosen a direction in which to move. Simultaneously, he says, he will take a peek at a few of his "indicating stocks"—which include JDSU and General Electric—

to make sure "nothing crazy is going on." Shortly thereafter, he takes a glance at CNN, to "make sure the government is still intact."

Cropley then proceeds to turn on his laptop, where he enters into a day trading chat room—an environment he describes as a good "social outlet." Since many day traders are pushing their own agendas, however, he is not keen on following the advice he receives from his chat room colleagues. "One thing I don't do is listen to them," he says. "I kind of play to the beat of my own drum."

By the time he is in and out of the chat room, it is just about time for the opening bell, and Cropley is scanning his various charts and indicators for potential plays. In the first half-hour, Cropley usually executes a couple of mock trades as he waits to see where the market is headed.

Around 10 A.M., he has obtained a feel for the market and is ready to enter some real orders. And by noon, says Cropley, he typically has closed out most—if not all—of the positions he entered in the morning. Then, somewhere in between noon and 1:30 P.M., Cropley takes a break for lunch, before jumping back in the market (around 2 P.M.) and finishing out his day.

Following the close of the market each day, Cropley prints out a summary of his trading activity. While scrutinizing the printout, he jots down notes on what he did right, what he did wrong, and what he could have done differently. "Even when I make money on a trade, I still evaluate it. I'll say to myself, 'I should have held longer, should have sold faster, or should have picked up more shares or . . . [fewer] shares,' " says Cropley. Such self-analysis, he says, is mandatory because it gives traders the insight they need to adjust their strategies on a day-to-day basis.

This said, sometimes all the analysis in the world is no substitute for being in the right place at the right time. Cropley's best trading day occurred in April 2000, when he took a flyer on the stock URMB. Conceding that he did not even know what that company does, Cropley says he purchased 1000 shares of URMB because his indicators looked good, and he figured he could "squeeze a few points" out of the stock. But then, to his surprise and delight, CNBC gave the stock a glowing review.

"CNBC, about 5 minutes after I bought it, pumps it. They say, 'Oh, my . . . , this is the stock to have. . . . So the . . . [stock] went up 20 points, and I had already [bought] around 1000 shares, . . . and I was just like, 'Sweet!' " says Cropley.

Still, while acknowledging that he was thrilled with his good fortune at the time, Cropley emphasizes that you cannot count on such big gainers. "A lot of guys live for the home runs, but . . . [the money] is not in the home runs—it's in the singles and the doubles," he says.

Calculating Risk

Traders who consistently go for the "home runs," of course, inherently are assuming greater risk than those who take small profits and small losses here and there. However, Cropley says that regardless of your risk-reward ratio, you must take precautions to protect yourself because—no matter how large your account—a string of bad losses could eliminate you. "Even if you have a million dollars [in capital] and you lose $500 on every trade, you're [eventually] going to run out of money," notes Cropley.

As part of his risk-management strategy, Cropley—who employs a 4:1 risk-reward ratio—maintains firm protective stops. Unlike the majority of his trading brethren, however, Cropley actually uses his direct access system to execute an automatic stop loss of $250 for each and every trade he makes. In other words, no matter what position he enters into, if his losses ever hit that magic $250 level, Cropley's system automatically exits the trade for him.

Cropley says that he chooses to use automatic stops because—in contrast to mental stops that most of his direct access colleagues use—they "take the emotion" out of trading. Consequently, he says, he never has to worry about a little voice in his head telling him to let a "gorgeous" stock, like JDSU, slip past his designated stop level. "I used to do analysis for each stock and think about how much capital I had in it, but the $250 [stop loss] seems to work perfect," he says. "It takes a lot of the thinking out of trading, . . . [and] it [was] easy to set up."

However, while he always uses a protective stop to eliminate potentially large losses, Cropley veers away from locking in profits through protective stops. "I've never used trailing stops, and I never really plan to," he asserts.

Typically, he says, he tries to let a winning stock "run 4 to 5 points" before closing out his position. Occasionally, however, he will lock in a portion of a winning position before he is ready to totally exit that stock—especially when the market is drawing to a close. "I will take some profit [at the close]. Even if my technical indicators aren't saying the stock is done yet. If we're coming to the end of the day, I will go ahead and close out [at least] half my positions," says Cropley.

To determine exactly where to exit a winning trade, Cropley pays close attention to a stock's intraday resistance and support levels. "I always draw trend lines for support and resistance," he says. "If you look at a chart and draw support and resistance lines, the stock just follows it, inside and outside." When feeling for an exit, Cropley also makes use of technical indicators, including a "stochastic" that illuminates when a stock is overbought or oversold.

Despite all the risk-management devices you may use, however, it is almost inevitable that you will someday come face to face with a string of losses. And when this happens, says Cropley, you have to step back and reevaluate your strategy. "I'm always fine-tuning my system, and it's gone through some radical changes," he says. "It sounds kind of cheesy, I know, like 'Chris Cropley's money making system.' But it really is important."

However, while Cropley believes he can reduce risk by adjusting his system in accordance with swings in the market, he does not subscribe to the theory that you can slash risk by spreading your short-term trading capital across multiple stocks. In fact, he says that if you keep multiple positions open at any one time, you could be significantly increasing your risk—because you are not going to be paying as much attention to any single stock you are trading. "Say you actively trade six stocks . . . [and] you're right two out of [every] three times. Well, then you [still have] two stocks that are going against you," Cropley explains.

Margin, of course, is one other risk factor that direct access traders must weigh. Cropley, for his part, says that since he has always traded on a 2:1 margin, his risk-reward ratio has been adjusted for that since his start in the direct access business. Moreover, he says that if you have a trading style that works, trading with borrowed money is no riskier than trading with your own capital.

Still, to offset any potential margin calls, Cropley says that he maintains some long-term positions in "large cap" stocks like GE and Microsoft. Emphasizing that he has yet to incur a margin call, he says that—rather than liquidating those positions to beef up the capital he can play with in his day trading account—he holds onto stocks like Microsoft to protect himself in the event that unlikely scenario unfolds.

Island Lover

Unquestionably, one way in which you can improve your risk-management scheme is by making smart execution choices. Cropley, for his part, loves to send orders to the Island ECN because it's fast and allows you to see the full depth of orders in its book. "I look at the Island book just as much as level II—because the market makers [on level II] will... [mess] with you," says Cropley. "Seeing all the bid and offers, [Island] shows you if the market makers are playing games with you, ... you can see if the stocks are really taking off or not."

Moreover, on Island, he says, he can compete for best prices and best executions with other day traders and online investors who trade through the likes of Ameritrade—instead of against "highly trained, highly paid" market makers. "I'll play against day traders and the Ameritrade... [users] and take their money," he says. "I try not to ... [make] the big boys [angry] ... because they are a little better than me."

To route a trade to Island, Cropley always uses CyBerCorp's intelligent order routing engine. The engine, Cropley says, is a very useful tool because it prevents him from exerting too much time and energy searching for the perfect execution destination. "It's really effective and enables me to focus more on the [actual] trade, [rather] than on spending time worrying about which order entry and routing system to use," he says.

CyBerCorp's smart order routing engine also allows Cropley to use either a low-ball or a high-ball strategy to go fishing for a point. For example, if Cropley is using a low-ball strategy, he may enter a buy order a point below the best bid—just to see if there are any matches out there. He can afford to do this, he says, because the CyBerCorp engine will scan the entire market for him—and will even occasionally find a fill. "And there's nothing better than getting filled on 500 shares for a point without doing a thing," declares Cropley.

Functionally, the intelligent order routing engine is supposed to automatically search all execution destinations (i.e., every ECN and every market maker) for the best match for your order. However, Cropley says that he has programmed his engine to scan the ECNs first, starting with Island. If the engine cannot find a match at an ECN, he says, it will then route an order to a market maker via Nasdaq's SOES network.

Per Cropley's command, the engine will not, however, route an order through Nasdaq's SelectNet pipeline. Cropley says he has "disabled" the engine's ability to link to SelectNet because, through personal experience, he has come to the conclusion that the system is "garbage."

Driving his point home, Cropley says that in one particular trade when he was shorting JDSU, SelectNet suffered a glitch that cost him a $1000 profit. "I shorted the stock, and I was like, 'OK, it's done.' ... The stock was about to turn back up, and I went to execute [a cover], and right before I did, I got a message that said 'SelectNet is down due to heavy traffic,' " Cropley explains. "And when I got back in, the show was over. . . . Any profit I was going to make was lost."

Regardless of the pipe he's routing an order through, Cropley almost always places limit orders. Traditionally, traders use limit orders to snag the very best prices. However, Cropley says that limit orders also come in very handy if a stock starts moving against you after you have shorted it. "If you're caught in a [bad] short, . . . you can offer a point better than the market is offering, [and] you'll get filled," says Cropley. "Somebody will be laughing . . . [as they go to] the bank, but at least you're not stuck on the market train."

Short Strategy

When the U.S. stock market hit a rough patch in the spring of 2000, Cropley decided that he needed to revamp his trading strategy to profit from the decline. Accordingly, he started using a short and cover strategy on a regular basis.

As a momentum player, Cropley figured that he would make money if he could find volatile stocks to trade—regardless of whether they were moving up or down. Consequently, he harbored no fear of the sell first, buy later approach.

Cropley, who holds a short position anywhere from a few minutes to 2 hours, says that he looks for stocks that display specific characteristics when he is shorting. For example, he says, if a stock shoots up 50 percent on a day when the market is in a decline, that stock is ripe for a short. "That's a pretty sure bet," he says.

Short sellers, he says, also should keep an eye out for stocks that are "taking off" based on "spurious news" and stocks that smack into their intraday resistance levels. "Once a stock hits that resistance, you know it's a good time to short," says Cropley.

Due to the unlimited risk factor associated with short selling, some short-term traders are leery of employing a short and cover strategy. However, Cropley says that he is not worried about a stock going on a bull run after he shorts it because he is monitoring that position very closely, and—most important—he has his automatic stop loss (of $250) in place. In addition, he says that his direct access system really simplifies life for him if wants to execute a short and cover instead of a buy and sell. "It's not a complicated process. You just use the sell button instead of the buy button, . . . and . . . [the system] automatically shorts a stock for you," Cropley explains.

Speaking of technology, Cropley's trading desk is configured with three computer screens: one screen to find stocks he wants to trade, one to analyze the stocks he finds, and one to execute a trade once he makes a decision to send an order. The first screen provides a broad market overview, displaying a list of the stocks Cropley is tracking and three charts: a 365-day, a Nasdaq Composite, and a Standard & Poor's futures index. The charts, Cropley explains, are displayed on the top half of the screen, and the lists are displayed on the bottom portion.

The second screen, meanwhile, contains a bevy of short-term charts, including 1-minute, 1-day, 5-minute, and 5-day charts. Lastly, the third monitor features Cropley's level II window and order-entry screen. With this monitor, Cropley can enter orders, receive fills, see what positions he has opened and closed, and view his real-time profit and loss (P&L) level.

Rules, Goals, and Advice

To keep his P&L in the black, Cropley adheres to a standard set of rules—including such oldies but goodies as do not hold stocks overnight, do not trade against a trend, and do not trade more than you can afford to lose. "I have the same generic rules as anyone else, . . . and I usually won't pay attention to someone else's rules unless I've read them somewhere else," says Cropley.

One other key rule, he says, is do not get emotional. But this rule, he says, can be very difficult to follow—especially if you are trading full time to support a family. For a family man, he says, dealing with huge market swings may be too stressful. "This is not for the faint of heart. It is not for people who have kids," he declares. "Even if I was really, really good, I don't think I'd be a full-time day trader if I had kids."

On a personal level, Cropley says that he has experienced the emotional trauma that comes with taking a big loss. In the spring of 2000, he recalls, he decided to go long one day on a couple of initial public offerings (IPOs). Unfortunately, he says, these IPO stocks went on a rapid decline, and he lost roughly $2500 in 3 minutes.

This experience helped Cropley realize that short-term online trading is far from a "get rich quick" scheme. To the contrary, he says, it is a very challenging profession that really "gets the juices flowing." "I have never sweated bullets before like I do in this line of work," he says. "You really have to be on your game, or you're going to get your . . . [butt] kicked."

However, the ultraconfident Cropley believes that, ultimately, he will be the one to administer a serious butt-kicking. In fact, Cropley predicts that in the not-so-distant future he will "master the challenge" of direct access trading. And when he does, he will move on to climb another mountain. "When this [direct access trading gig] gets to be old hat and I become a Jedi Master, then I will find something else to do," he boldly prognosticates.

MARGARET DECKER: SPEECH PATHOLOGIST TURNED MOMENTUM TRADER

From October 1999 until March 2000, Margaret Decker raked in an average profit of between $7000 and $10,000 per month. Working as a full-time direct access trader, Decker—a former speech pathologist and a current grandmother of seven—had just about brought her life full circle.

When she was a child, Decker recalls, her father used to watch programs such as "Wall Street Week" and frequently talked about his portfolio of stocks. As the years passed and she grew into a young adult, she started to read the *Wall Street Journal* and became very interested in the business of investing. "While other women [I knew] bought the *Ladies Home Journal,* I bought *BusinessWeek,*" Decker recollects. "But I didn't go into the [stock trading] field because it was not a field that women went into at that time."

Now, however, at age 60, Decker is enjoying a new career as a short-term online stock trader who executes transactions via a sophisticated CyBerCorp-supplied trading system. Although she initially incurred significant losses when she began her direct access career in early 1999, Decker recovered (with the aid of her October to March windfall) and is currently making a prosperous living.

However, while she undoubtedly made her dad proud, Decker certainly took a circuitous route to get where she is today. She got married, had kids, and then launched her career back in 1984—when she obtained a master's of science degree from the University of Washington.

Shortly after graduating from the university, Decker started working as a rehabilitation consultant in the speech pathology field. Roughly 13 years later, she grew weary of the travel her job required and decided to take a year off to manage an IRA account she had set up with the online brokerage firm Charles Schwab.

By her own account, she did "pretty well" trading her IRA through Schwab. However, she wanted greater control of her trades and faster executions. Therefore, in January 1999, she began using MB Trading's Real Tick III direct access system. Just 6 months after that, searching for better technology and "superior customer service," she says she migrated her direct access account from MB Trading to CyBerCorp.

Direct access technology, says Decker, has given her more control over the time aspect of her trades. Moreover, it has eliminated the need for her to worry about "lag time" when her trades are being reported.

At the same time, however, she cautions that short-term online trading is only for people who want to be the driving force behind every trade they make. Essentially, she says, when you migrate to a direct access system, you have to "become your own broker"—a job that requires you to both fashion your own trading style and keep a vigilant eye on your stock portfolio.

Riding Momentum

Decker describes herself as a combination of a momentum player and a swing trader. Lately, however, she has used momentum as the catalyst for 100 percent of her trades. Basically, all this means is that she will only trade a stock that is actively moving (either up or down).

Beyond the volatility factor, however, there are also a number of other criteria Decker has in place for each trade. For example, she will only trade a stock with an intraday volume of at least 500,000 shares. And the maximum she is willing to lose on any single trade is $250.

Decker, who makes an average of 10 trades per day, also aims to rake in between $500 and $1000 in profits on a daily basis. Typically, she keeps a position open anywhere between 2 minutes and a half a day, and she determines her share size based on the price of the stock she wants to trade.

Decker will buy (or sell) 1000 shares of a stock priced $15 and under, 500 shares of stocks priced between $15 and $30, and 200 shares of stocks priced between $30 and $80. The smaller the share size, the larger the number of points Decker is looking to grab. For instance, with a 200-share order, Decker wants to net a profit of at least 1 point. Moreover, she says she is willing to hold on to such positions for a bit longer than larger-sized orders. "It's those high-priced movers that go and go, and you make a lot of money," Decker explains.

With regard to order entry, Decker has a set price in mind before she jumps into a position—but she is willing to chase a stock ¼ point beyond her ideal entry price. If she cannot get her stock within ¼ point of her ideal entry price, she will just wait for a better opportunity to come along.

Before entering a position, Decker takes a look at how the futures indexes (the Nasdaq Composite and Standard & Poor's) are performing. In addition, she analyzes a variety of technical indicators, including a stochastic (which tracks the relationship between a stock's last closing price and its intraday high/low), candlesticks (which highlight the difference between opening and closing prices), and the relative strength index (which measures the strength of a stock based on changes in its recent closing prices).

On a regular basis, Decker keeps an eye on a list of "15 to 20 stocks." Emphasizing that she does not trade all these stocks every day, Decker says that she monitors stocks from different sectors—so that she can immediately get in on the action if one particular sector gets hot.

Indeed, before she finalizes her decision on which stock she is going to trade, Decker tries to locate a sector where stocks are really moving. Right now, she says, the most volatile stocks reside in the technology sector. Decker, who also tries to trade stocks in her price range ($15 to $80), says that her current list of favorites include JDSU, Sun Microsystems, Cisco Systems, Oracle Corp., and Amazon.com.

Regardless of the stocks she is trading, however, Decker never has more than two positions open at the same time. Moreover, if she is trading a "very active stock," she will only keep one position open.

Leveraging Level II

One of the things that can define your failure or success as a direct access trader is your ability to read—and analyze—a Nasdaq level II screen. Fortunately, says Decker, she has become fairly adept dissecting level II data. "If I watch the level II, and watch the time and sales [window], I can just about tell you when a stock is going to turn," she says.

Although it is not actually integrated into the level II screen, the time and sales window (usually located adjacent to level II) is important because it gives you a pretty clear read on whether traders are pumping or dumping the stock. However, Decker says that the very first piece of data she eyes when she opens a level II screen is the bid column. "I first want to know what the bids are . . . and who is in the inside bid or ask," she says.

As she is watching prices move on level II, Decker is checking out the number of levels there are on the bid and the ask and is monitoring specific market makers to measure how frequently they jump back and forth between those columns. "If there are not a lot of sellers and there's a lot of buyers, I know the stock is going to go long," says Decker. "And you may as well get in when it's going up and get your point, because it's not going to go up forever."

In addition to providing you with the data you need to make a decision about whether you should buy or short, the level II screen can unveil valuable information about a stock's resistance and support levels. And this information, if used properly, can help you decide where to get out. "If you see a lot of buyers . . . and you can see one point down there's a lot of sellers, you know that about all you're going to get out of . . . [that stock] is between ½ point and 1 point," explains Decker.

To pinpoint exactly when to go long or sell short, Decker also tries to identify the market maker who is "running the show" for the stock displayed on the level II screen. Once she identifies the leader of the pack, she tracks the individual movements of that market maker in a stock box window she has set up on her computer screen.

Slashing Risk

Like other successful direct access traders, Decker recognizes the importance of risk management. To this end, she follows a group of risk guidelines. For example, she sets a strict protective stop loss so that she never loses more than $250 in any single trade. Moreover, she refuses to risk more than 20 percent of her capital in any one trade.

If she does suffer a loss, Decker typically will vacate her post for a moment, go down to her kitchen, and grab a cup of coffee. This process, she says, helps her keep her emotions in check. Moreover, to maintain a positive frame of mind, Decker analyzes losses in points instead of in dollars. "I don't think about the money aspect [of a loss], because that gets you trapped," she says. If she did think in terms of dollars, Decker adds, she might try to "get revenge" to make up for her losses.

In terms of trailing stops, Decker says that she will only lock in portions of her orders if she is trading a sizable amount of shares. For example, if she has already made 4 points on a 1000-share buy order for a stock that is moving quickly, she will use a trailing stop. "If I have a stock that is going way up, when it gets to the top of the RSI, I'll sell half my shares. . . . But I won't [sell a portion of my shares] with a 200-share order," says Decker.

Similar to the majority of her trading brethren, she borrows money to trade to add to her leverage. But Decker—who trades with the aid of a 2:1 margin 50 percent of the time—says that trading on margin only really increases your risk factor if you take home positions overnight.

Occasionally, Decker says, she does take home a position after the close. However, if she decides to hold a position overnight, to decrease her risk, she will not carry over a losing stock or a stock that is known for its volatility. Moreover, she says her 20 percent capital rule protects her from incurring any margin calls.

To protect against a series of losses, she adds, it is also important to have a "good mental attitude" and avoid partying the night before trading. "You have to be alert, . . . [and] your mind has to be in the right condition to trade," Decker emphasizes.

Of course, a trader's execution destination choice also can have an impact on risk. Decker says that she sends orders directly to an ECN 90 percent of the time. Island, she says, is her favorite ECN because it is easy to use, has the most liquidity, and allows her to trade directly against other individual investors (instead of market makers). "When you trade on Island, you have more control over what you do," she says. What's more, Decker says Island is superior to other execution destinations in terms of the speed at which it delivers fills.

Every once in a while Decker will rely on CyBerCorp's intelligent order routing engine to find an execution point. And although she avoids SOES, she will, on rare occasions, route an order via Nasdaq's SelectNet.

However, Decker claims that she will only use one of Nasdaq's order-routing pipes if she wants to exit a position really quickly and "doesn't care" how much that exit will cost her. "If there is no one on Island who will buy the stock [I'm selling], and I want to get out, I send a market order . . . through SelectNet," she explains.

As of August of 2000, 70 percent of Decker's total orders were shorts. On average, she keeps a short position open anywhere from 5 minutes to 2 days. However, to ameliorate her risk, Decker is increasingly shying away from holding shorts overnight. "I've held . . . [short positions] at times overnight because I knew the stock was going to go down, and it did. But I wouldn't do that now [in August]; the market is too crazy," says Decker.

Ideally, when she makes use of a short and cover strategy, Decker wants to find stocks that are overbought. One way in which she determines this is by scanning the market for stocks that are "getting toppy"—or wavering as they hit their resistance lines.

In truth, Decker's current love of the short game was born out of necessity. She began shorting frequently, she says, back in March and April of 2000 when the Nasdaq market was in the midst of a significant decline. At that time, says Decker, shorting was "the only way you could survive."

However, as it turns out, Decker gained invaluable insight into the nature of the market through her "survival" experience. For example, she learned that stocks that shoot up very fast come down just as quickly. And those fast-moving stocks are exactly the types of securities Decker wants to trade.

Early Riser

Every trading day Decker wakes up in the morning to the sound of National Public Radio, takes a shower, has breakfast, and flips on CNBC by 7 A.M. Then she takes a peek at the futures indexes (Nasdaq Composite and Standard & Poor's) and taps into online business news services—such as the *Wall Street Journal* and CBS MarketWatch.

After she gets her fill of news, she hops into KingCambo.com—a day trading chat room—to see if any stocks are being seriously hyped. Simultaneously, Decker is monitoring her stock list to see if any of her stocks are experiencing significant volatility in the premarket. Occasionally, Decker will send an order directly to Island before the open, especially if she pinpoints a stock that is moving (either up or down) in the ECN's order book.

At the open, she says, she is keeping a particularly keen eye out for stocks that have gapped up significantly—because she knows that they will tumble down eventually and that they therefore make good short plays. However vigilantly she is monitoring the market, though, she takes a cautious approach, waiting until after 10 A.M. to begin inputting her orders. "Sometimes it's crazy to get in [at the open] because you've got market orders from last night, the market makers are throwing their stuff in, and you don't really know what's real. . . . So I just let all the fools get out of the way [before getting started]," she says.

From 10 to 11:30 A.M., Decker is very active in the market. During that time period, she eyes two separate 17-inch monitors that contain a wide variety of data and trading tools. On the data end, Decker can view a dynamic ticker, a top 10 volume list for stocks trading on both Nasdaq and the NYSE, and a host of different charts. On one of the screens, she also has a window that gives her access to the Island book—through which she can see all the open orders and all the orders that have been executed on the ECN.

With regard to trading tools, Decker has an alerts feature (that informs her when certain stocks are ripe for a buy or a short) and—of course—the all-important Nasdaq level II window. Besides displaying all the pertinent information she needs to make an informed trading decision, the level II window is also tied to an order-entry device that allows Decker to execute a trade with the simple point and click of a mouse.

In the first half of the day, most of her trading activity takes place within 2 hours of the open. Indeed, from 11:30 A.M. to 1:30 P.M., during the period Decker calls "the dead zone," she hardly makes any noise. Following lunch, however, Decker jumps back into the market (between 2:15 and 2:30 P.M. at the latest).

Toward the close, she says, she is looking for short plays with a quick turnaround potential. As the clock ticks closer to 4 P.M., says Decker, more and more professional day traders are looking to close out their positions. Consequently, she says, the closer it gets toward the end of the day, the more opportunities there are to short—as long as you act fast.

In the first hour after the close, says Decker, there are also some good short-term opportunities. The companies that are particularly appealing during this time frame are the ones that have just released earnings reports. Typically, says Decker, companies that do not have "fabulous blowout earnings with fantastic revenues" see their stocks take a dip. And those declines, she says, lead to some "really fantastic" short plays. This said, however, Decker cautions that trading in the after hours market is probably a little too volatile for the beginning direct access trader.

Daily Journal and Rules to Live By

As part of her ongoing effort to stay ahead of the curve and keep her account in the black, Decker also maintains a daily trading journal. "I write down what the [Standard & Poor's] futures are at 8:00 in the morning, what they are at the open, and what the psychology of the market is. . . . Then I write down the stocks I will trade that day. When I enter a short, I write down the entering price. And when I close them, I write down the cover price, and then I calculate the profit," explains Decker.

Noting that she keeps all this information in a Quicken spreadsheet, she says she usually analyzes her journal entries after the close, to determine what she did right and what she did wrong. At times, however, she says, she has even searched through journal entries that date back an entire year. "Right now, I'm going back to last year and seeing that the same patterns that happened last year are happening this year," says Decker. The trading journal, she adds, also comes in handy when she gets her account statement from her direct access broker and needs to verify her trades.

Peeking into the future, Decker says she wants to start trading options—and increase her share size when she is trading stocks. "I would like to increase my point average so that I can consistently make $1000 a day," she says.

Meeting this goal will not be easy. However, to help move toward it, Decker says that she will continue to follow a few well-known rules: Do not trade against a trend, do not attempt to get "revenge" on a stock, and do not enter a market order for a stock that is issuing an IPO. Undoubtedly, these guidelines do not carry the same weight with all direct access traders, but for Decker, breaking these rules is not an option. "When I don't go by my rules, I lose," she concludes.

JERRY PARNHAM: MOMENTUM TRADER TAKES FLIGHT

Jerry Parnham, a direct access trader who buys and sells stocks from his home office in Wafilla, Alaska, believes that online trading is very similar to flying an airplane. In either endeavor, he notes, you are destined to crash and burn—unless you receive proper training. And Parnham, a 49-year-old graduate of the University of Minnesota, should know. When he's not banging away on his computer keyboard trading stocks, Parnham works as a pilot, flying 747 jets for Northwest Airlines.

Of course, prior to catching on with Northwest in 1986, Parnham built up a tremendous knowledge of flying—through both education and real-world experience. Parnham's flight education really began following his graduation from high school, when he spent 2 years at an aviation mechanics school. After acquiring an aviation mechanic's license, Parnham enlisted in the Air Force, where he worked as an aircraft mechanic. Then, following his stint in the Air Force, Parnham went back to school, graduating with a degree in aeronautics from the University of Minnesota. Shortly thereafter, he began piloting commuter airplanes before ultimately starting his own aerial crop spraying business (his last stop before North-west).

Similarly, nearly 2 years ago, Parnham set out to get thoroughly ed-ucated before beginning a career as a direct access trader. He learned about the pros and cons of short-term online trading by reading several books, and then—after deciding he wanted to give direct access trading a shot—he enrolled in a week-long trading "boot camp" hosted by a training firm called the Online Trading Academy.

Held in Irvine, California, the boot camp gave Parnham an enlight-ening overview of the intricacies of Nasdaq level II. Moreover, the boot camp delivered important insight on the ins and outs of a variety of execution systems. "I can't advocate enough getting educated. . . . If I hadn't gone to day trading academy, I would have gotten burnt out," says Parnham.

Not surprisingly, Parnham had to cough up $2000 to attend the boot camp—but that money was refunded to him after he agreed to open an account with CyBerCorp, a direct access broker. After signing up with CyBerCorp in the spring of 1999, Parnham used the broker's technology to execute mock paper trades for 3 months.

Then, in July 1999, Parnham started using CyBerCorp's software to trade for real. Unfortunately, he says, he quickly realized it was much easier to trade on paper than in the live market. One distinct difference is that whereas you always get a fill when you are performing a mock trade, you do not get automatic fills when you are trading for real.

Initially, Parnham ran into a brick wall. In fact, in his first 3 months using a direct access trading system he lost roughly half the capital with which he started his CyBerCorp account ($15,000 in cash and $30,000 in margin). However, instead of knocking him out of the business, those initial losses increased Parnham's resolve to succeed. And from Novem-ber 1999 until March 2000, Parnham did just that, raking in $54,000 in net profits. Moreover, during that same period, he claims he never lost more than $250 in a single day.

Parnham—a momentum trader who enters between 150 and 200 or-ders a day—attributes his initial struggles to his failure to trade via a systematic plan. During his first 3 months, he says, he often would go for "big wins" without thinking about the risk-reward ramifications of those trades. However, Parnham's fortunes began to turn around when he decided that he would live by a specific set of rules and approach each trade with a specific plan in mind.

Strategic Evolution

In his quest to develop a successful plan, the first step Parnham took was to devise a formula for determining share size. After giving the subject some thought, Parnham decided that the price of the stock he was interested in would determine the number of shares he traded. For example, for stocks priced $10 and under, he would buy (or short) 1000 shares; stocks priced in the $10 to $20 range, meanwhile, merited a 500-share order; and lastly, stocks in the $20 to $100 range rated a 200-share order.

Similarly, Parnham decided to base his risk-reward ratio on the number of shares he planned to buy or sell. For example, for a 1000-share order, Parnham's goal is to make a minimum of ¼ point; for 500 shares, his profit goal is ½ point or more; and for 200 shares, he wants to snag a gain of at least 1 point. His maximum risk level, Parnham decided, would be the same as his profit goals (¼ point for 1000-share orders, ½ point for 500 shares, and 1 point for 200 shares).

Such price- and size-driven techniques, he says, enable him to avoid tying up his whole trading portfolio in "one or two or three stocks." What's more, these techniques steer Parnham toward his profit goal of $1000 per day.

Of course, before he makes any money, Parnham—who keeps positions open anywhere from "10 seconds to all day"—must select the stocks he wants to trade. Although he uses various methods to select his stocks, one thing he steadfastly believes in is that momentum traders must subscribe to a good chat line.

As an individual, Parnham notes, you may be able to keep tabs on 10 to 20 stocks throughout the course of a day. However, if you get on a good chat line (Parnham's favorite is KingCambo.com), you will benefit from having "100 pairs of eyes watching 1000 stocks."

Parnham cautions that you have to choose your chat line wisely because some traders use these vehicles only to "pump a stock" before dumping it. However, with all those eyes perusing the markets, Parnham occasionally receives exactly what he is searching for—tips on stocks that are poised for either a big run or a long slide. "I don't care about what the name of the stock is, what they sell, or what their financial position is. All I care about is if it's moving up or down," he says.

After figuring out the direction in which a specific stock is going to move, Parnham enters a position using a low-ball, high-ball strategy. Depending on whether he is going long or short, Parnham tries to enter a position ½ point below or above the inside bid or inside ask for a stock listed on the level II screen. For instance, if he is shorting, he will enter a sell order ½ point above the best quote in the ask column. In contrast, when he is buying, he will enter an order a ½ point below the inside bid—or "low ball" that bid.

The activity taking place on the level II screen, Parnham says, enables him to determine exactly when and where to enter a position. While scanning level II, Parnham determines who the "heavy hitters" are by examining the share size being posted by the different market makers. Just as significantly, he is looking to see whether the market makers are lined up on the bid or the ask side. "The biggest thing is the number of shares on the bid side. If you've got a lot of market maker orders [lined up] on the bid side, [then you know] the price is going down," he says.

On top of the quotes and share size posted by market makers, Parnham says that level II watchers also have to keep an eye on the amount of volume a stock has generated during the course of a day. At the online trading seminar, Parnham says, he was taught to look for stocks with at least 100,000 shares in volume—but he personally prefers to trade stocks with volume levels of "several hundred thousand shares."

All in all, following the direction of a stock is a lot simpler if you can dissect a level II screen. Parnham, in fact, says that his ability to read and analyze level II has given him the power to accurately predict the direction in which a stock is going to move. However, he also emphasizes that becoming a level II wizard is something that can only be achieved through real-world experience.

From Premarket to Postmarket

Although Parnham wakes up at 4 A.M. (Alaska time) each trading day to get ready for the opening of the Nasdaq, his preparation really begins the night before. Following the close of each trading day, Parnham accesses his email account and pulls up the CBS "After Markets Report." Searching for stocks to trade the following day, he scans the report—which is delivered to his email free of charge every trading day—for about an hour.

Eventually, he culls a list of 10 to 15 stocks from that report, separating the potential short plays from the potential long plays. Then, when he awakens bright and early in the morning, he checks that list of stocks and scans the market for other high-volatility securities. Sometimes, Parnham says, a stock is experiencing volatility as a result of news—either good or bad.

Summing up his premarket strategy, he declares that he is simply "just looking for something that's moving." Not surprisingly, one of his favorite premarket stocks to play is JDSU, a security that lately has been subject to significant after hours price movement. "This thing will [typically] gap up 3 points in the morning. I'll buy it long [in the premarket], ride it up a point or 2, and [then] at the open, I'll short it, because I know it's going to go down," explains Parnham. "Two weeks ago, JDSU went up 8 points [prior to the open]. I shorted it at the open, and followed it down 5.5 points in 15 minutes."

As part of his premarket routine, Parnham also turns on CNBC and taps into the Island ECN's after hours order book on his laptop. Through that book, he says, he can get a quick glance at the 20 stocks generating the most volume in the after hours market.

At the open, he says, he is searching for stocks that have gapped up significantly in the premarket. For example, he says, a good short candidate may be a stock that gaps up 10 points prior to the start of trading because it is the product of false bandwagon hype. Such stocks, says Parnham, are bound to "come back down to earth" and thus represent short plays that are usually good for anywhere from 1 to 3 points.

Typically, Parnham enters about half his orders in the first hour of the trading day, shorting stocks that have gapped up. Although he keeps a close eye out for any stocks that have experienced breakouts or breakdowns throughout the course of the day, Parnham usually avoids trading between noon and 1 P.M. because there is little activity in Nasdaq stocks.

Parnham's trading activity usually heats back up again toward the close—especially during the last 30 minutes of the day. At that time, he says, the market is ripe with possibilities because market makers are scurrying to "cover their orders." Following the close, Parnham occasionally will put in orders in the postmarket. However, he cautions that you have to be careful because there are usually only a handful of stocks that are moving during that time period.

Playing the Short Game

In the first 8 months or so of his foray into the world of direct access trading, the majority of Parnham's orders were of the traditional "buy low, sell high" variety. In March 2000, however, when the market took a significant turn for the worse, Parnham decided that he needed to adjust his strategy.

To take advantage of the declining market, Parnham started short selling on a frequent basis. This short and cover strategy worked extremely well, he says, at a time when the market "went to hell." In fact, Parnham says, in the middle of the market decline, he experienced his best month ever, raking in roughly $20,000 in profit in March.

During this market decline, Parnham realized that stocks have a tendency to fall faster than they do to rise up. And the success he achieved gave him extreme confidence in his ability to consistently wind up on the winning side of short plays. Short selling, in fact, has become Parnham's preferred style of trading. At the time we interviewed him (July 2000), 75 percent of the trades he entered were shorts.

To determine whether to use a short and cover or a buy and sell strategy, Parnham relies on Bollinger bands—a type of indicator that measures the volatility level of a stock. "They are phenomenal. . . . They tell you when you should buy and when you should short," he says. "Market makers use them, . . . [and] I have them on all my stocks."

To avoid any unnecessary risk when shorting, Parnham tries to close out all his positions on an intraday basis. Unfortunately, he says, he has in the past held stocks overnight that have turned against him. At times, Parnham says, he has gotten burned by riding his "gut" feeling. "You end up with what I call pigs in a blanket," he says. "Those are stocks which are wrapped up in a blanket of your money."

Holding an overnight position, adds Parnham, is the one way in which a short seller can run himself or herself out of business—especially if the short seller does not have a huge wad of capital as back up in the event the stock he or she is carrying over takes a sudden and dramatic turn upward.

However, while you must take steps to protect your capital while shorting, there are also a few things that you must remember in order to maximize your profits. For example, Parnham says, any stock that doubles in value has very good short potential—because it will likely "decrease by half" the amount it jumped up.

Moreover, Parnham says that stocks priced under $10 that break through their resistance level are also nice short candidates. "I know from experience that a stock (under) $10 isn't going to run that many points. So while everybody else is jumping on, and they are buying, buying, buying, I'll look for the peak—I'll look for it to waver at the top—and then I'll short it and follow it down," he says.

Placing Mental Stops

Although he has the ability to input automatic stop losses for every trade he makes via his direct access system, Parnham only uses mental stops. By using mental stops, he says, he can adjust his stop loss level if a Nasdaq level II screen is indicating that the stock is "about to turn." In contrast, if you have an automatic stop loss of, say, a ½ point, once the stock reaches that level, your system will automatically exit the position for you.

This said, Parnham does believe firmly in setting stop losses. When he started direct access trading and did not have mental stops in place, Parnham says, he did not exit his positions quickly enough. Consequently, he says, in one of his early direct access excursions, he took a $4000 loss—the most money he has lost, cumulatively, in a single day. "I was going long and stayed in the stocks too long, . . . [and] I didn't use a mental stop loss," Parnham explains.

After experiencing his worst day, Parnham decided that he would curb his risk by putting a $1000 limit on the total amount he was willing to lose on any given day. And to this day, he says, if he hits this $1000 loss ceiling, he "walks away" for that day. "If I'm having a bad day, I'll shut it down and go do something else. . . . Tomorrow's another day," theorizes Parnham.

The problem that many new traders encounter is going for the "home run" instead of taking "singles and doubles," says Parnham. Going exclusively for the big gainers, he says, is a sure-fire way to "burn up your trading portfolio" to the point of no return.

To reduce risk, says Parnham, traders also must remember to never lose sight of what is going on in an open position. "If I have an active trade going on, I never leave my screen," he says.

Of course, you also can limit your risk and enhance your profit potential by choosing an appropriate execution destination. Parnham says that he routes more than 90 percent of his orders directly to the Island ECN for execution. By doing so, he says, he can "set his own price" and cancel an order "at will."

This said, if he is not happy with what he can get over Island, or if he feels that he needs to exit a position regardless of whether he is getting his desired price, Parnham will, on occasion, use CyBerCorp's intelligent order routing system. As we have noted before, this system automatically seeks out the best price among all the different ECNs and market makers.

However, Parnham says that he uses his smart order routing technology for only about 5 percent of his orders because the software conceivably could cause your order to get hung up in the SOES network. "The smart key can take 30 seconds, and in the meantime, your stock can be diving or tanking and moving against you," cautions Parnham.

Regardless of whether he is sending an order directly to an ECN or searching for a destination through the intelligent order routing software, Parnham says that he always uses a limit order. Market orders, he says, are easy pickings for market makers and therefore should "absolutely never" be used by short-term online traders.

Similarly, Parnham says that active traders must always remain focused and thus should avoid monitoring a large group of stocks simultaneously. "I never have more than three open positions going at the same time. That's all I can watch at one time," he says.

Screen Setup

In his office, Parnham has three 17-inch PCs lined up next to each other. Spread across these monitors are four charts: one that tracks the intraday movement of a stock, one that reveals the 365-day cycle of a stock, one that highlights the Nasdaq Composite index, and one that features the Standard & Poor's futures index.

On one of his monitors he has a stock box that displays pertinent information about the stocks he is interested in trading—including the number of points those stocks have gained or lost intraday and the intraday highs and lows for those stocks. This box, says Parnham, can be integrated with your charts. "You can tie your charts into your stock box so that when you put a stock symbol in [the stock box], it automatically displays that stock on your charts," he says.

Next to his Nasdaq level II windows, Parnham also has a box that displays the Island ECN's order book. "The market makers will tell you if a stock is going to move, but also the day traders will tell you on the Island book what the stock is going to do," he says. "The Island book and the level II are right next to each other, and it's amazing how they work together."

Parnham's trio of screens also features various other bells and whistles, including a dynamic ticker, a personal account manager, and a real-time P&L window. The dynamic ticker displays real-time prices for the stocks Parnham is interested in, the personal account manager keeps him updated on the status of his open positions, and the real-time P&L tracks Parnham's intraday profits and losses.

Final Thoughts

At the end of each one of his daily trading sessions, Parnham prints out a summary of his trading activity. The summary—which is supplied by his direct access broker—illuminates the amount of money he made, the percentage of winners and losers he traded, the total commissions he paid, and the percentage of stocks he bought versus shorted. However, although Parnham does give the summary a once-over, he does not spend a lot time studying it because when he makes a mistake, he says, he now knows almost immediately when and why he "screwed up."

Fortunately for Parnham, his mistakes lately have been few and far between. Indeed, he has come a long way since his pre-direct access trading days, when he was making 2 percent interest—after taxes—on a money market account and thinking to himself, "There has got be a better way to make my money work for me."

Even though he lost nearly half his initial $15,000 account in his first few months as a direct access trader, Parnham now has more than $50,000 in his CyBerCorp account ($100,000, with margin). What is more, he says that he has made up to $5200 in a single day.

In part, he says, his success as a direct access trader can be attributed to his quiet life—which includes "no wife, no kids, and no worries." On a personal level, this means that he has no real distractions while he is trading. "To successfully day trade, you have to concentrate [fully] on what you are doing. . . . You can't have any interruptions," Parnham declares.

However, despite Parnham's success, people interested in jumping into the direct access game should not be under any delusions that they are going to get rich fast. As Parnham can personally attest, new direct access traders are almost guaranteed to take their share of lumps. The real key to staying afloat, he says, is to limit your initial losses and learn from your mistakes.

RICK DUMNICK: FROM DRUMMER TO DIRECT ACCESS TRADER

Back in the 1970s, when Rick Dumnick was just a young boy, his grandfather taught him a valuable lesson about the U.S. stock market. While keeping an eye on an old-fashioned stock ticker, Rick's grandfather—who emigrated from Italy to America—suggested that he and the boy play a little game. The elder Dumnick then told Rick to give him a dollar in exchange for a piece of paper. After the exchange, Grandpa Dumnick told Rick that he could sell him back the piece of paper at any time but also explained to him that the value of the piece of paper could rise or fall depending on the direction in which the ticker moved. The ticker then scrolled up, and the elderly Dumnick told the boy that he could make some money if he sold him back the piece of paper. "He said, 'If you give me the piece of paper back, I'll give you $1.25.' I said 'No, I'm going to hang onto it.' He said 'Okay, it's [worth] $1.50 now. Do you want the $1.50?' And I said, 'No, no. I'll hang onto it,' " Dumnick recalls, "I waited, and then [the value of the piece of paper] started to go down. It went down to $1.25 again, and I got disappointed. Then I got mad and said I'm [still] going to hang onto it."

Unfortunately, the piece of paper continued to dwindle in value, falling to $1 and then, finally, all the way down to 25 cents. "I wound up . . . losing 75 cents of my $1 allowance," the grown-up Dumnick remembers with a chuckle. That day, Rick's experience with his grandfather not only got him interested in the stock market but also made him realize the importance of risk management. After all, had he been wise enough to know when to say when, he would have snagged a sizable profit instead of taking a big loss. Despite learning about the intricacies of the stock market at such an early age, however, it would be more than 20 years before Dumnick considered making his living as a trader.

In the mid-1980s, Dumnick enrolled at Palm Beach Community College in Florida, where he initially pursued a business degree. Shortly after starting school, however, he had a change of heart and decided that he wanted to make music his major. He honed his talent and became a pretty decent musician, playing a mixture of jazz, rock, and "fusion" on his instrument of choice—the drums. In fact, he even did some professional studio and session work for a while. However, a neck injury forced him out of the professional percussionist business. And when that window of opportunity closed, his evolution toward full-time online trading began.

Initially, Dumnick opened a traditional brokerage account with Smith Barney, buying and selling stocks with the assistance of his financial adviser. At that time, he says, he was using a position-trading strategy, jumping in and out of stocks in a "2-week to 2-month" time period. To boost his knowledge of the equity markets, he would read stock charts and printouts sent to him by his adviser. Moreover, around that same time, Dumnick began surfing the finance sector of America Online to pick up useful stock trading tips.

Then, in the mid-1990s, thanks in part to his experience surfing AOL, Dumnick decided it would be wise to open up an online brokerage account with Bank of America (BOA). He took what he learned from position trading and attempted to trade stocks on a much more short-term basis, maintaining open positions for an average of 5 minutes to 1 hour. Eventually, however, Dumnick became disenchanted with BOA and decided to try out a cheaper online discount broker. However, after spending only a short amount of time as a client of SureTrade, he was unhappy with the speed of the service he was receiving and decided to close his account.

Finally, in 1999, Dumnick hopped on the direct access bandwagon when he opened an account with CyBerCorp. Today, Dumnick, age 34, uses CyBerCorp's trading system to trade from his home office in Boca Raton, Florida. In 1999, as a full-time online trader, Dumnick says he netted profits of more than $100,000. Dumnick declines to provide a rough estimate of his P&L for the year 2000 but asserts that it has not been as prosperous as 1999.

The Search for Trends

Dumnick hardly ever scalps and rarely holds onto positions after the close of the market because too many negative things (such as a bad earnings report) can happen overnight. Although he does not like to pigeonhole himself as any specific type of trader, he acknowledges that he tries to trade stocks that are moving with strong momentum in either direction. Specifically, Dumnick prefers to trade stocks in the technology sector because stocks in that sector are historically "very volatile" and tend to follow trends. "I'm looking for stocks that go up when the market goes up or down when the market goes down. . . . I want something that shows a little bit of predictability or exceptional strength," he explains.

On average, Dumnick strives to make between 2 and 10 points per trade and typically holds onto a position anywhere from 5 minutes to 2 hours. In terms of price, he says that late last year he traded stocks in the $10 to $60 range. Now, however, Dumnick trades stocks priced at $100 and up—primarily because those stocks are subject to significantly wider price fluctuations than the cheaper stocks. "As opposed to, say, last December, when [day traders] were trading the cheaper stocks, . . . now they seem to be congregated in these more expensive stocks. I would guess that's because there's a lot more volatility [in the expensive stocks], and they can trade less shares and still have significant point moves, like [between] 10 and 20," he says.

Since he now pursues more expensive stocks, Dumnick has had to significantly reduce his share size. Whereas he used to trade between 1000 and 5000 shares, he says, he is now trading between 100 and 500 shares.

Two of the stocks Dumnick currently trades in his reduced-share increments are Redback and Rambus. Both those stocks have the volatility that Dumnick craves and are part of a stock list that he regularly scans in his quest for winners. Dumnick says that his stock list serves two purposes: (1) it keeps him abreast of stocks that meet his criteria for trading, and (2) it reduces the chance that he will make a play for a stock he knows little or nothing about.

On average, Dumnick says, he makes about $2500 on winning days and waves goodbye to $300 on losing days. However, Dumnick says that he does not use any mathematical formulas to calculate his risk-reward ratio. Instead, for each trade he makes, he simply asks himself how much chance the stock has of moving against his position compared with for his position. To determine the answer to this question, Dumnick says, he looks at different charts and indicators—including the moving average of a stock.

Rick's Trading Rituals

On a typical day, Dumnick wakes up around 7 A.M., has some breakfast, and does a little bit of reading. After he is done reading, around 8 A.M., he turns on CNBC on the TV and begins to make notes of trends and news he should keep an eye out for during the course of the day. Simultaneously, he takes a peek at a chart displaying the Standard & Poor's futures index and periodically checks back prior to the opening bell to see if he can get a read on whether the Nasdaq is going to have a strong or a weak opening.

Fifteen minutes before the opening bell, Dumnick boots his computer up and starts analyzing different charts. His favorite is the 5-minute bar chart, but depending on his view of the volatility in the market, he also may pull up 1-minute bar charts for specific stocks. Simultaneously, he keeps his ears tuned to CNBC to make sure he does not miss out on any market-changing announcements. "I'm looking for any kind of windfall-type news, be it good or bad. If there's a bad earnings report, I may take a look at that particular stock and make a very quick preliminary analysis of it, and I might decide to get in on something like that. I [also] watch for interviews with CEOs and CFOs of companies that I've heard about on the news quite a bit," he says.

After he analyzes all his chart information, he zones in on two or three specific stocks in which he has strong interest in trading that day. Flipping through this short group of stocks, he is trying to pinpoint the one that has "a definite direction in relation to the market."

Following the opening, Dumnick continues to monitor his target stock for "at least 5 or 10 minutes" to evaluate how it is responding to the changing market conditions. Once he finds a stock with a strong pattern formation, he then calls it up on his level II window. And then he starts intensely scrutinizing the movements of the market makers in that stock. "In level II, a lot of times you'll see market makers lined up on one side or the other. Usually, when you see that type of a thing, you'll see the ECNs lined up on the other," he says. "The marker makers are pulling the stock in one direction. So, if they're on the bid side, they're pulling it down. If they're on the ask, they're pulling it up. Or [at least] they're trying to."

Beyond paying close attention to the moves of market makers on level II, Dumnick is also looking for a stock that is nearing the bottom of a Bollinger band on a chart. "If I'm going long . . . and I'm 99 percent sure this thing is going to go up, I want to buy it near the bottom. I don't want to buy it near the middle because that's an indication that the people who are in the stock are very unsure,' he says.

If the market is trending upward at the open, Dumnick will attempt to long the stock that he is interested in at the end of that stock's initial pullback. "I'll wait for the first pullback and try to enter at that point. Then I'll probably exit at the top of the second [pullback], when I see the stock either rounding out or [entering] another congestion area."

Naturally, if the market looks like it is going to trend downward at the open, Dumnick will employ a short strategy. However, he says that you must do your homework on stocks, because a stock that looks like a potential short candidate may gap up a little bit at the open. A stock may still be a good candidate for a short if, for example, the market is overreacting to a resistance level the stock broke through near the close of the day yesterday.

Most of Dumnick's trades take place between 9:30 and 11 A.M. Dumnick says that he likes to enter and exit trades in the morning because that is when the market is starting to set patterns for the entire day.

Moreover, there is a great sense of optimism if the market opens strong. "You tend to see greater moves in the morning because people are expecting things. They're expecting a good day. If you find a good long play and the market is in good form, . . . [investors] are more likely to jump onto . . . [the stock] and take the ride," he says.

Dumnick says that he never keeps more than one position open at a time because it is too difficult for him to watch a bunch of different stocks simultaneously. Moreover, he says that he tries to keep an extremely close eye on the position he does have open—particularly if he carries that position into lunchtime (11:30 A.M. to 1:30 P.M. in the day trading world).

Back in 1996, in his pre-direct access days, Dumnick left a position open when he went out to lunch. He had held that position for 2 weeks and was trying to extract a 10-point gain from it, he recalls. However, when he returned from lunch—to his ultimate horror—he noticed that the stock was down $25,000.

That experience may have soured Rick on trading in the afternoon. Today, citing the fact that the session is mentally taxing, he says he rarely trades the close. In fact, most of the time, Dumnick closes out all his positions prior to lunch. "By noon, sometimes, I'm just tired out and don't care to continue," he says.

The Art of the Short Sell
Unlike some active online traders, Dumnick is just as willing to engage in a short sell as he is to take a long position. He says that he keeps a list of between "three and five stocks" that look like potentially good shorts. Ideally, Dumnick wants to find a stock that has been oversold in a downward-trending market. "On a down day in the market, I would automatically go to my short list and say, 'Okay, let's see which stock is performing the . . . [worst],' because obviously only one is going to drop the most," he says.

Finding the stock with the greatest downward momentum, says Dumnick, is the only way to make any real money in a bearish market because most or all of the other stocks in its sector also will be falling. Dumnick says that he does not pay too much attention to late-breaking bad news in a downward market because even though that news may add momentum to a stock's fall, it does not push it out of control. Rather, he says, he looks for the weakest of a weak group of stocks.

This said, while he prefers to short weak stocks in a downward-trending market, Dumnick says that it is possible to find good short can-

didates in an ascending bull market. Stocks that are suffering from recently released bad earnings reports, he says, are the best targets for shorts
when the market is on an upswing. "If you have bad news on a stock in
an up market, . . . that [stock] tends to plummet fairly quickly. Everything
else is in such a positive light that when you have some kind of [negative]
news, . . . it will go [down] sometimes twice as fast as it would normally,"
says Dumnick. However, he emphasizes that you have to act fast if you
are going to short a stock with bad earnings in a bull market because
such stocks have a tendency to fall rapidly.

Trading stocks that have just released negative earnings reports is also
one way in which you can reduce your risk while shorting. Dumnick says
that since bad earnings news is usually going to cause a stock to decline
for an extended period of time, you are a lot less likely to take a loss if
you short that type of stock.

In a perfect world, he says, he will short a stock suffering from bad
earnings at the top of its decline. However, he warns that you have to be
careful because you can never be certain when a stock will suddenly
"correct" itself in the midst of a fall. "When you see it start to turn
around, the first time it goes against you, you can just dump that stock.
. . . Find something better, and just replace it," Dumnick advises.

For his part, Dumnick does not buy into the argument that short plays
are more of a gamble than long plays. While acknowledging that short
sellers have to face an unlimited risk factor, he says that if you apply
"proper technical and fundamental analysis" to your trades, shorting really is not any riskier than going long.

In terms of minimizing risk, Dumnick says that you must always
remember to only short a stock when it is moving downward. "Don't
look for a stock that's trending upward and decide you're going to short
it. That's the worst possible mistake you could make. Then you run into
that scenario where it could just go upward to infinity," he cautions.

Stop-Loss Techniques

Like most direct access traders, Dumnick maintains a mental stop loss
for each and every trade he makes. However, he does not decide what
that stop-loss level will be until he actually enters a trade. Moreover, after
figuring out what kind of stop he should use, he evaluates whether he
should adjust his stop loss on a stock-by-stock basis. "Say I got in at 52
and the stock goes up to 60 and I say, 'Okay, I'm going to have half a
point mental stop loss on this thing. . . . If it comes down to 59½, then I

might say, 'Okay, it hit my stop loss,' but then I'll look and make a quick assessment [of the stock's momentum] using the level II window," says Dumnick. "And then I say to myself, 'All right, either I can still get 60 for this thing . . . or I'll just take the 59½ and get out.' "

To decide whether he should lock in his profits on a winning trade, Dumnick looks to see if the stock has hit any "congestion areas." When he is riding a winner and sees that the stock has hit a point where it is showing some clear hesitation, he will exit the trade. For example, if a stock moves up 8 points but then suddenly starts "clicking back and forth" in a 1-point range, Dumnick will sell—especially if he sees that trend occurring two or three times within a 1- or 5-minute bar chart.

Going into each trade—just as he has no preset notion about the amount of profit he would like to lock in—Dumnick has no maximum stop loss in mind. If a stock is moving against him, he says that he will put in a limit order to try to stop the bleeding. The one thing he will not do is enter automatic stop losses. Anyone who relies on his direct access software to input automatic stops is just asking for trouble, says Dumnick. "If the stock happens to dip below [your stop-loss] price, then . . . [your system] will [automatically] execute at the market, and you could be in trouble. So I try to avoid that," he explains.

Since he relies on his evaluation of chart patterns to determine when he is going to jump in and out of a stock, Dumnick also does not use preset entry and exit price parameters. "You can't really predict a chart pattern . . . until it happens," he says. "Stocks tend to either move below or above a moving average. This can kind of detract from the idea of having a set entry point and set exit point."

If he were to determine an exit point prior to making a trade, Dumnick fears that he could lock himself out of a very profitable trade. "What I'm really doing is just ignoring everything like . . . [exit targets]. I have no clue where a stock is going to go when it starts to head upward. All I know is I want to get in at the bottom and let it go upward," he says.

Kudos to Island
One way in which Dumnick successfully snags stocks near the bottom is by routing orders to the Island ECN. In fact, roughly 80 percent of his orders are sent directly to Island. Most of the time, Dumnick says, Island has the price he is looking for, and the ECN provides very good fills.

There are times, however, when Dumnick must use an alternative to the direct ECN access approach. If, for example, he wants to trade a high-priced stock that is moving rapidly, he may not be able to find the ECN quote he wants quickly enough. Thus, in such situations, he relies on CyBerCorp's smart order routing system to make up his mind for him. Around 15 percent of the time, says Dumnick, he relies on the smart order routing system to find the best execution destination. The system works by automatically scanning all market makers and ECNs for the best bid or offer available at the price and share size a customer specifies for a stock. The system comes in particularly handy, says Dumnick, in high-pressure situations that call for you to "either make up your mind or forget the whole trade."

This praise not withstanding, Dumnick warns that you have to exercise a little caution when using a smart order routing system because it is simply searching for the best price. When it finds that best price, it will route the order to that destination—even if it means sending an order to a market maker through SOES.

And given the fact that he got burned playing the waiting game on SOES in the past, Dumnick says that he tries to avoid that system as much as possible. "The thing about SOES is that a market maker has 30 seconds to decide whether he [or she] wants to move your order or not. In a fast-moving stock, 30 seconds is like an eternity, and you can't close the order. Once the thing is open, the . . . [marker maker] has 30 seconds to decide. He [or she] is in control. It's on his [or her] screen. Nobody else is seeing it. If you preference it to him [or her], nobody else is seeing that, and it could lock things up," he says.

To avoid having his limit order tied up in SOES, Dumnick says that when he uses the smart order routing system, he tries to make sure that there are two or three ECNs lined up on the bid or offer for the stock he is chasing. If he does not want to send an order directly to Island and is worried about experiencing delays using the smart order routing system, Dumnick says that he sends an order to a specific market maker through SelectNet.

On the rare occasions when he does use SelectNet (around 5 percent of the time), Dumnick is not concerned about the fact that he has to wait at least 10 seconds before canceling his order. "If I'm using SelectNet, it's for some specific reason. Maybe I just don't want people to see [that] I'm putting a large order in, and I don't want anyone to see it except for that particular market maker. If that's the case, then the market is slow enough that I'm not concerned about 10 seconds anyway," Dumnick explains.

Regardless of the order-routing mechanism he chooses, Dumnick uses limit orders almost exclusively. Market orders, he says, are too dangerous. "A market order can get tied up. That could be hanging out there in the open and just sitting there, and nobody wants to take it. And since it's a market order, if you have 100 people in front of you, you could end up waiting half the day," Dumnick says.

If you want to get out of a stock, instead on inputting a market order, Dumnick recommends that you input a limit order for the second or third best quote you see on your level II screen. "If you're buying, go for the second or third best ask; if you're selling, go for the second or third best bid, and try to avoid the smaller moves. Don't worry about ⅛ or 1/16 of a point. . . . Look for stocks that are moving, that you expect to move several points, and then use the fractions to your advantage in order to get in there quickly and get back out quickly," Dumnick advises.

Risk Management

The first rule of risk management, says Dumnick, is to do all that you can to try to enter into a long position near the bottom. Getting in near the bottom, he says, is "really a lot more simple than most people make it out to be." Unfortunately, he says that traders constantly make the mistake of not trusting formations they see in their bar charts—even when they indicate that a stock has gone through a downward spiral and is beginning to show resistance. "The stock's starting to form a round bottom, . . . [but] traders tend to still be careful. They don't have the confidence to jump in yet. And then when the stock starts some sort of an upward motion, they jump in," Dumnick says.

What often ends up happening, he says, is that traders chase a stock up until it reaches the top part of the first pullback, and then they buy. "What they end up doing is they sell it at the bottom of the first pullback, [before] the thing takes off again. That's the biggest mistake that most people make. I see so many people doing that, even professional traders," he says.

Aside from buying low, you must exit a trade quickly if the stock starts to move against you. "Cut your losses and get out. If you lose $500, that's fine, because you might make $5000 or $10,000 on the next trade," Dumnick theorizes. Traders who are riding losing streaks, he says, must be able to "take a breather and reassess" the market and the specific stocks they are trading.

Personally, when Dumnick experiences a string of consecutive losses, he takes a couple of days off and tries to clear his head. Then, when his mind is "completely off the market" and he has pushed all of his worries aside about how he is going to pay his bills and preserve his capital, he will bring his stock charts up one evening and reevaluate them. "I'll look at anywhere from a 1-minute to a monthly [chart], looking for patterns. Sometimes you get a more overall view with, say, a 60-minute chart as opposed to a 5-minute chart, and sometimes that's really all it takes to see the general trend," he says. "I might see an upward trend that I didn't see on a 5-minute chart, and maybe I was [mistakenly] shorting the stock the whole time."

Dumnick says that you will be able to spot trends, and consequently minimize risk, if you pay close attention to a stock's resistance and support levels. "I try to buy near support and sell near resistance. If you have a trend happening and you draw these support/resistance lines and buy it near support, chances are [that] probably at least 80 percent of the time, the thing is going to go up. If it violates that line, it's probable that it will still reestablish, and that's where stop losses come into effect," he says.

One last factor to consider when you are mapping out your risk-management strategy is the practice of margin trading. Dumnick says that borrowing money from your broker to leverage your account has its pros and cons. On the plus side, he says, margin gives you the power to buy twice as many shares as you normally would. On the downside, he notes, you could end up losing twice the amount of the total capital you have in your account—if the stock moves against you, and you face a margin call. However, while asserting that he would not recommend trading on margin for traders who have just opened their first direct access account, Dumnick says that he never worries about getting a margin call. This carefree attitude, he says, is due in large part to the fact that he almost never holds positions overnight.

On the subject of making a living via short-term online trading, Dumnick says that one of the great benefits full-time direct access traders enjoy is the "peace of mind" that comes with knowing your orders are going to be executed properly. "Where the real advantage comes in is that I get instant confirmation. . . . [Fills are] instantly posted to my account, and it's instantly liquidated and my profits are posted," he says.

Still, even with sophisticated direct access technology on your side, Dumnick says that good, old-fashioned discipline is still the key to trading success. "You're not always going to win, but if you keep the losses to a minimum and you look for larger moves, then you should be okay," Dumnick concludes.

ELI BURSTEIN: MEET MR. MICROTREND

Eli Burstein leads a busy life. Although he maintains a full-time job at a start-up information technology consulting firm, Burstein somehow finds time to make an average of 15 to 20 trades per day. What is more, he executes these transactions by employing a strategy that calls for him to religiously track the movements of only a pair of stocks: JDS Uniphase (JDSU) and Exodus Communications (EXDS).

In fact, since he trades JDSU and EXDS almost exclusively, he has had to study feverishly to build up his knowledge of the market markers that trade these two stocks. Despite the fact that this part-time passion seriously eats into his social life, Burstein—a self-proclaimed "microtrend trader"—is invigorated by his analytical approach to trading. "It is exciting to monitor stocks closely, to really learn their intricacies and be able to capitalize on those," he says.

By gaining "expert" knowledge of the moves of market makers that trade JDSU (a supplier of fiberoptics products targeted at the telecommunications and cable television industries) and EXDS (a provider of Internet-based network management applications), Burstein says he now can quickly recognize different intraday trends in these two stocks. And such recognition, of course, can lead to the ultimate goal of every direct access trader—big-time profit.

However, before he made any real money, Burstein—a recent graduate of the University of Pennsylvania who only began trading through a direct access system in January 2000—embarked on a trading adventure. Eventually, as a result of that journey, Burstein completely scaled the evolutionary trading ladder, climbing his way from investor to casual trader to direct access trader.

A few years back, at the start of his sojourn, he opened an account with Charles Schwab, one of the original online brokerage firms. Shortly thereafter, however, he started trading more often and decided to transfer his trading capital to Datek Online Brokerage Services—a relatively new entrant in the Internet-based brokerage business.

Unfortunately, Datek could not provide a trading panacea for Burstein. One problem, he says, is that he could not get access to Nasdaq level II through Datek. In fact, to get level II quotes, he had to subscribe to a separate service called Windows on Wall Street. "It became quite pricey. And some of the direct access firms . . . [were] offering all that in a single, bundled package," Burstein recalls.

What is more, whereas Datek only offered its clients an indirect gateway to one ECN (Island, in which it owns a majority stake), a direct access broker could provide fast direct access to multiple ECNs. And since multiple ECNs actively place bids and offers for the stocks he trades, Burstein ultimately decided that he needed to upgrade to a bundled direct access system on which he could see all the ECNs on level II.

To this end, in January 2000, Burstein transferred his trading capital to an account with the direct access broker Tradescape Securities. Via Tradescape, Burstein finally was able to obtain a system that not only could deliver faster executions but also could provide all the key data and quote information he needed through a single trading screen.

Prior to making the switch to Tradescape, Burstein read a few books and did some research online. Still, like most inexperienced direct access traders, Burstein struggled through his first couple of months. However, while declining to provide specific details about his initial hard luck, Burstein says that he increased his trading capital by roughly 20 percent within his first 6 months of direct access trading.

Style Profile

On an active trading day, Burstein holds a position for an average of 40 minutes and trades anywhere between 75 and 100 shares. While he has a definite idea about the number of shares he is going to trade and the amount of time he would like to hold a position, Burstein does not incorporate preset entry and exit price targets into his systematic trading plan. "When I recognize something that I feel should trigger an action, I'll take that action," he explains. "At any given time, I might see [that] somebody is trading large shares or doing something aggressive, and I might think that's an opportunity to buy."

To determine his entry point, Burstein peruses the quotes being posted by ECNs and market makers on his level II window (which we will discuss in detail later on in this chapter). In addition, he says that he maintains "very thorough charting" on the positions he is holding. However, while he actively monitors intraday charts and occasionally peruses charts from the previous day, Burstein says that it is important to avoid getting "too historical" when you are analyzing stocks. If you try to follow weekly charts, for example, you can "inundate yourself" with reams of unimportant data, says Burstein.

For similar reasons, Burstein does not believe in the practice of maintaining a daily trading diary. Keeping a log of your daily activity, he says, is much too cumbersome for typical direct access players. Moreover, he says that since active traders cover "a limited number of stocks," they instinctively store a great amount of pertinent data about those securities in their memory banks.

Burstein needs to tap into that memory bank most frequently at the close of the market—his most active period of the day. As the market moves toward the finish line, more bids and offers are placed by ECNs, and consequently, there are more "bargains" to be found, says Burstein. "I'm significantly more active at the close. I find that everything is much more liquid then," he says. "Volumes tend to increase . . . [because] a lot of people are looking to either curtail or extend their positions."

No matter which period of the day he is trading in, Burstein usually tries to get in on the long side of a stock. Most of his profits are made, he says, after he enters a buy order during a bull market.

Just Say No to Shorts

Part of the reason Burstein subscribes so heavily to the traditional buy/ sell approach is because of his distaste for the short game. If you are scalping for "small gains here and there" and using stop-loss orders, says Burstein, then shorting is really not any riskier than going long. However, he emphasizes that if you are keeping positions for a longer period of time, you will incur more risk—because you are more susceptible to a short moving against you. "If you hold your positions a little longer, as I sometimes do, then . . . [shorting is] a lot riskier," says Burstein.

In fact, he says, he experienced his worst trading day while executing a short and cover strategy. A few months back, Burstein says that he was shorting the stock INKT (Inktomi Corp., a supplier of scalable Internet infrastructure software) on a volatile day in a declining market. All the other stocks in the sector (Internet infrastructure) were trending downward, he recalls, so Burstein decided to short INKT early and often. Initially, he says, he did fairly well, scalping the stock for small gains. But then the tide turned. "The stock turned around and had an up day when the rest of the market was down," Burstein explains. "I believed it was going to follow the suit of the other stocks in its sector, and I kept shorting it with more blocks . . . to basically try and cover other losses I had incurred earlier."

By feverishly attempting to recover the money he had lost, Burstein— who had shorted INKT more than 30 times during the course of the day— let his emotions get in the way of rational decision making. The end result: INKT closed on an upswing, and Burstein wound up losing 12 percent of the money he had invested in trades for that stock.

Today, on the rare occasions when he does short, Burstein searches for sectors that have plummeted in a declining market and tries to find the stocks that have taken the worst hits. Within each sector, he says, he is looking for one stock that "really stands out"—one that is completely devoid of any good news.

Level II: The Great Equalizer

The one window that always "stands out" on every direct access trader's PC is level II. For many short-term online investors who trade on behalf of their own accounts, the level II price display window serves as a tool that helps level the playing field against professional traders.

In Burstein's case, the first piece of data that catches his eye on the level II screen is the depth of the bid column. Once you see the depth of the bids, he says, you can draw conclusions about the market demand for a stock. However, Burstein, who is also eyeing the share size that is attached to the different bids, says that the most vital data that level II offers is the market maker quotes. "That's where I feel I can really benefit because I've tracked these securities [that I trade] for a really long time, and I feel [that] I can anticipate the moves of the market makers who deal in these stocks," he says.

Mainly, says Burstein, he is looking for "consistency across market makers" in the stocks he trades. If every market maker is pushing a stock in a specific direction, then he or she will try to follow that trend and ride its coattails. Moreover, if Burstein sees a "pronounced trend across multiple market makers" trading a single security, he will even trade stocks outside the pair (JDSU and EXDS) he trades on a daily basis.

This said, while he pays close attention to the market makers to gauge the direction in which a stock is moving (and, in some cases, to determine which stocks he is going to trade), when it comes time to enter an actual order, Burstein searches for the best ECN quote available on level II. ECNs, he says, represent the execution destinations where the "most reliable prices" can be found. Therefore, they also are the market centers where direct access traders are most likely to get their orders filled.

Rather than focusing on one ECN, he says that most short-term players are scanning level II for all the different ECN quotes that are posted for a single stock. While asserting that he typically executes his orders through a trio of ECNs (Archipelago, Instinet, and Island), Burstein says that he tries not to focus on a single execution destination—because no individual ECN is going to determine the "risk factor" for a stock.

Speaking of risk, some traders also pay close attention to the volume data displayed on the level II screen to help them determine whether a stock is liquid enough for them to trade in. However, the volume listed on level II is of little significance to Burstein.

Noting that volume data are important to a lot of traders who trade large blocks of stock, Burstein says that his average share size is too small to merit him paying much attention to volume. "I don't have enough cash to acquire huge blocks, so volume doesn't mean much to me," says Burstein. However, he adds that he does expect to pay much closer attention to volume a "couple of years down the road" when he has more capital to work with and can afford to scalp more.

Similar to the volume data, a stock's historical information holds little importance for Burstein. Since scalpers are generating much of intraday volume for active stocks, he says, having intimate knowledge of the historical resistance and support levels of those securities does not deliver any real advantage to a trader.

Knowing a stock's intraday resistance and support levels, on the other hand, can certainly boost a short-term trader's success ratio. And one way in which Burstein keeps tabs on real-time resistance and support levels is by monitoring intraday stock charts. On an active trading day, Burstein says that he is "constantly" viewing and analyzing intraday stock charts—adjusting his trading strategy whenever he sees trends emerging.

What is more, he is also searching for intraday trends among stocks traded in the same sector. Burstein, whose favorite stock sector is Internet infrastructure, says that he looks for any stocks that are lagging behind others in a sector that is on an upswing. If a stock is trailing others in its sector without good reason (e.g., bad news), Burstein says that it is an excellent candidate for a buy. "With a lot of stocks, the market makers will follow the sector trends and then act accordingly. So, if you can preempt . . . [the market makers] by a couple of minutes here and there, you're almost defining the market for that stock," explains Burstein. "Unfortunately, however, the market makers usually jump in there a little more quickly than I do."

Stops and Equity Allocation

Just as learning how to read and analyze a level II screen is key to any direct access trader's success, so too is the ability to curb losses through

managing risk. For many traders, establishing a protective stop-loss level
is one of the first steps taken in the development of an effective risk-
management strategy.

Although he adjusts his stop loss on a stock-to-stock basis, Burstein
says that he "always" uses a protective stop and "always" sets it so that
he never loses more than "4 to 5 percent" of his total account equity.
Usually Burstein does not choose the exact price at which he is going to
employ a stop prior to taking a position in a stock. Rather, after he enters
a position, he determines his protective stop based on the number of
points he expects a stock to move during the time he plans to hold it.

At times, Burstein also uses trailing stops to secure a slice of his
profits. Typically, he will not enter a trailing stop if he is only going to
keep a position open for a couple of minutes. However, he will enter a
trailer if he is riding a winner and has no immediate plans to exit that
trade. "If I'm going to hold a position a bit longer, I'll enter a trailing
stop to lock up the profits that I have made," says Burstein.

If he chose to, Burstein could have his direct access system automatically input a protective stop each time he makes a trade. Like most
of his trading brethren, however, Burstein prefers to use a manual stop
loss. Mainly, he says, he follows the manual/mental approach because of
the penchant he has for adjusting his protective stop level.

Aside from using protective stops, Burstein also maintains a high
"account equity" to reduce his risk. On a daily basis, he does not let his
account equity (or trading capital) dip below 80 percent of what he started
the day with. By sticking to this guideline, he says, he eliminates his need
to worry about margin calls and increases the time he can hold on to
stocks that have not performed as expected. "Before you pick your stocks
to trade, you have got to do your due diligence. And if you like a particular stock and it's had a down time and you maintain a high account
equity, you can afford to wait [a while] for it to turn around. And I find
that the stock often will do that," says Burstein.

From a share-size perspective, Burstein weighs the trading capital he
has invested in open positions and the length of time he is planning to
hold those positions before deciding how many shares of a specific stock
he is going to buy or short. "If I'm maintaining a longer position in a
given security, and my account equity is going to stay low for a little bit
of time, then obviously the sizes of my active trading blocks are going
to go down," he says. In contrast, says Burstein, if he is a holding a liquid
position that he feels he can exit at any time, he would be more likely

to increase his share size—because he could cover any losses he might incur in the new position by "liquidating" his open position.

On top of keeping his losses to a minimum, Burstein's share-size and account-equity guidelines also enable him to avoid margin calls. Like just about every other direct access trader, Burstein does trade on margin—but he always limits his borrowing to a 1:1 ratio. In other words, if he buys $1000 worth of stock with his own capital, he borrows a maximum of $1000 to increase his capital investment in that stock.

In the past, Burstein says borrowing too much money has stung him. For example, when he had an account with the online broker Datek Holdings, he was "maxing out" his margin rights and—as a result—was periodically getting margin calls for "small sums of money." Tired of taking losses, he says, he reduced his borrowing ratio (from 2:1 to 1:1) and started religiously following the old adage "Never trade more than you can afford to lose."

One way in which Burstein tries to ensure that he adheres to this adage is by holding long-term positions. Completely separate from his short-term trading account, Burstein says, he maintains a long-term "investment portfolio." Since he can always "fall back" on his long-term holdings in case he has an "emergency" with any of his short-term positions, Burstein says his long-term account gives him an extra layer of risk protection.

Moreover, in addition to providing a security blanket, his long-term holdings provide Burstein with an option to be a little more aggressive. "If I ever . . . [made a trade] that I just loved, and decided to deviate from my rules, and then ended up getting burnt on it, I'd still be okay. I wouldn't be jumping out of any windows because I'd still have that veritable savings account outside my active trading account," he says.

However, while Burstein does subscribe to various risk-management theories, he does not believe you can slash your risk by either (1) spreading your trading capital across a plethora of stocks or (2) pulling out of the market temporarily after a string of losses.

In terms of spreading out your trading capital, Burstein says that active traders who do so actually may be increasing their risk because they are not focused enough to catch all the important details—such as market maker movements—for each stock they are trading. "If you're an active trader making multiple trades a day with high-liquidity stocks, then there is no real reason to diversify. In fact, I think diversification is almost a negative in terms of the prospect of [all of the information] overwhelming you," says Burstein. In contrast, he says, if you accumulate intimate knowledge of just a few stocks, you can capitalize on the trends occurring within those securities.

Separately, he says that traders who take a break from the market after incurring a series of losses are making a mistake. Rather than bailing out of the market, Burstein says, traders who stumble into the multiple-loss scenario simply should decrease their share size and make a couple of trades to regain their confidence. If you have been successful in the past, he emphasizes, you cannot let a few consecutive losses knock you out of the market. "If you have a sound understanding of the market and the stocks you are trading, . . . then you have to trust yourself. You've to got to dance with the girl who brought you," says Burstein.

ECNs: There Is No Substitute

When it comes to executing a buy or sell order, Burstein always "dances" with ECNs. For Burstein, order routing is all about finding the ECN that has the best quote for the stock he is trading. While asserting that he does not have a favorite ECN, he says that he often has found very good quotes on Island.

Island's parent, Burstein notes, is Datek Holdings—an online brokerage firm that caters to an audience comprised largely of part-time traders who trade on a fairly irregular basis. And since many of the Datek traders route their orders to Island, Burstein says, you can find some "good bargains" on the ECN that you "can't find anywhere else."

Due to the fact that he has always sent orders directly to ECNs, Burstein has never used either SelectNet or SOES—and he does not think that he will use Nasdaq's order-routing technology in the future. "I just haven't felt the need to go directly to the market makers," says Burstein. "Any time I want to execute an order, I feel I can get . . . [a fill] by routing it directly to an ECN."

While he never uses SelectNet or SOES, Burstein also rarely uses the smart order routing system that comes as part of his direct access package from Tradescape. The smart order routing engine, he says, is beneficial for traders who spread their capital across a bunch of stocks—because they may not have the time to find the best price for each stock, and the Tradescape engine will do that work for them.

However, given the small number of stocks that he actively trades, Burstein says, the engine offers no real benefit to him. What is more, he says that he gets a "better feel for the market" when he searches for the best price himself. "I have played with . . . [the smart order routing system] and I find that it is very reliable, but I just prefer to keep an eye on everything myself," says Burstein.

Still, regardless of which ECN he ultimately sends an order to, he always uses limit orders. Although he advises against using market orders at all times, Burstein says that if you absolutely need to use one, use it on the sell side of a winning trade. "A market order is not going to kill you . . . [if] you've already made money on the stock. . . . [But] on the buy side, I think a market order is definitely just a mistake," he says.

One other mistake that a direct access trader could make is to place a market order at the open. Such a move, says Burstein, would defy all risk-management logic because the market order would be exposed to everyone who trades at the open. Consequently, he says, the trader who enters that market order would stand virtually no chance at exiting the trade at a decent price.

Guiding Lights

All in all, it is fair to say that Burstein believes that direct access traders should never enter a market order at the open. And, as we already discussed, Burstein always uses a protective stop and always maintains 80 percent of his account equity. However, he also lives by one other rule: Always research a stock before you start actively trading it.

Before you begin trading a security, he says, you should get a "feel" for its intraday trends. And the best way to expose these trends, says Burstein, is to research the market makers who trade that stock. "A lot of people will just happen onto a stock and say, 'The volume looks good, and I can scalp it for a $\frac{1}{16}$ here and there,' and then they start trading it. . . . But you should spend weeks, if possible, really researching the market on that stock before you do that," he says.

Indeed, Burstein himself spent a lot of time researching the two stocks he now actively trades before he started trading those securities. What is more, he says that on the rare occasions when he has deviated from his own rule on research, he has had bad results.

Speaking of negative results, holding losing stocks after the close of the market is one strategy that is infamous for getting traders into trouble. Indeed, wary of the dangers of keeping positions open overnight, Burstein says he rarely engages in this practice—even when he is holding winning stocks near the end of the day. "You never know what they're going to announce after the close," Burstein warns.

However, Burstein thinks that—the dangers of holding overnight not-withstanding—the biggest mistake that direct access traders make is "overextending themselves" after they make consecutive winning trades. Too often, he says, traders increase their share size when they are riding a profit wave—diverging from the winning formula that propelled them to success. "You have to maintain some degree of consistency and level-headedness when you are up," Burstein cautions.

Unfortunately, he says, this is easier said than done. Indeed, Burstein pleads guilty to overextending himself on occasion. "I've been in and out of a stock that I just love and then said to myself, 'Okay, let me increase my share size,'" he recollects. "That [causes me] to deviate from any strategy that I have established, and there is much more significant potential for a downside because my account equity dips."

Above all else, he adds, direct access traders must remember the following: You cannot win all the time. "You're going to have days when you lose a lot of money. It's just the nature of what we are doing. . . . [And] if you're not willing to acknowledge that and you want every trade to make you money and every day to yield a profit, you're not going to be very satisfied," Burstein concludes.

EDDIE HERNANDEZ: MAKING THE TRANSITION FROM COMMODITIES TO STOCKS

Early in the year 2000, after working as a successful commodities trader on the floor of the New York Mercantile Exchange (NYMEX) for the past decade, Eddie Hernandez decided it was time to try something new. Thus, backed by the cash he made trading gold, sugar, cotton, crude oil, and coffee options, Hernandez jumped into the realm of direct access trading. Although it was very different from the frenetic, face-to-face driven trading he grew accustomed to while working in the open-outcry pits of the NYMEX, Hernandez quickly learned that direct access trading of stocks and auction-style trading of commodities were bound together by at least one common theme: Nothing beats experience.

Indeed, the experience factor actually persuaded Hernandez to abandon direct access trading in favor of a more lucrative opportunity trading gold after only his first month on the job. "If there is a busy market in commodities right now, I can make more money in 1 day then I can in 3 months of day trading," he explains. "So when gold took off, I stopped [trading stocks] and went back into gold for about 6 months."

However, in June, Hernandez found himself back in front of his direct access trading screen. Earlier in the year Hernandez had agreed to become a partner at Zahr Securities, the broker/dealer affiliate of Zahr Trading, the commodities trading firm that had given him his start all the way back in 1988. Thus, when Zahr Securities made its official debut in June, Hernandez—who is now one of seven equal partners at the firm—decided that it was time to get back into the stock trading game.

Even though he had vast trading experience, Hernandez—like most other first-time direct access traders—initially struggled to make a profit. In fact, it took him around 2 months (from June to August) to reach the break-even level. And despite the fact that he reached break-even faster than most beginning direct access traders, Hernandez says that his first 8 weeks on his new job reminded him of how important experience truly is.

"When people come into . . . [Zahr's] office, I tell them that they should expect to lose money for [the first] 3 to 6 months," says Hernandez. With this in mind, Hernandez advises new traders who join Zahr's office to "take an average of how much you're willing to lose [per month] and then set goals off that."

After achieving his first goal (to break even), Hernandez set a profit goal of $500 per day. "Once I was doing that consistently, my goal was to make $1000 per day. And after that, it was $2000, and that's where I'm at today," he says. The more experience he gained, he says, the easier it was to reach his net profit plateau. For example, he says, after he started consistently taking home $500 a day, it only took him 2 weeks to jump to $1000. Moreover, he says that recently he made $15,000 in a day— his high as a direct access trader.

This said, while experience can serve as the great equalizer for a trader, it also does not hurt to be a little lucky on occasion. After graduating from Iona College in 1988, Hernandez decided against pursuing any type of job in the field of his major—computer science. Instead, he chased after a job in the commodities market, where his brother worked.

Subsequently, Hernandez got a job as a clerk at Zahr Trading, the commodities firm that operates on the floor of the NYMEX. Roughly 1 year later, he says, Zahr promoted him to a position as a trader. Soon after he received his trading badge, the Persian Gulf War was launched, and as luck would have it, the first instruments Hernandez traded were crude oil options. "Shortly after I started trading, the Gulf War broke out. I was trading crude oil, and that was probably the best time to be a commodity trader," Hernandez recalls. "So even though I was relatively new, I did pretty well." Hernandez felt fortunate that after a year of clerking, he got thrown into a very busy market that was "kind of giving money away."

Following his fast start trading crude oil options, Hernandez went on to build a lucrative career trading gold, sugar, cotton, and coffee options. However, beyond the financial incentives, Hernandez says he was lured into the world of commodities trading because of the flexibility the job offered him. Typically, he says, he would go into work between 9 and 9:30 A.M., leave by 3 P.M., and arrive home between 4 and 5 P.M., giving him plenty of time to spend with his wife and children. Moreover, he did not have to wear a suit to work and could take it relatively easy on days when the commodities market was dead.

Speaking of dying, Hernandez says that one of the reasons the partners at Zahr Securities launched the broker/dealer service was because the company felt that Zahr Trading's open-outcry-driven trading business was becoming obsolete. Zahr Trading, he notes, relies on floor-based trading, but the commodities industry is shifting toward fully automated trading. "There is still some money to be made in the pits, but I think eventually it will be all electronic," Hernandez says.

Today, Hernandez trades out of Zahr Securities' office at One North End Avenue in New York. Zahr's facility, he says, is equipped with a Watcher Technologies–supplied direct access trading system and caters to both proprietary traders (who trade on behalf of the firm's account) and nonproprietary traders (who trade for themselves). Hernandez falls into the former category. However, he says that because he is a partner at Zahr, and because the firm does not make markets in stocks, he is essentially trading with his own money—just like the nonproprietary traders who work in Zahr's office.

Searching for Momentum
Hernandez, who likes to trade stocks in the price range of $50 to $150, describes himself as a momentum trader who is typically in and out of a position within 2 minutes. He usually makes around 100 trades per day, at an average of 400 shares per trade. Gradually, as he becomes more successful, he expects to increase his order size. "As I see my P&L growing, I get more comfortable with [larger] size," he says.

Ideally, Hernandez wants to trade a stock that fluctuates no more than $5 to $15 during the course of a day with a tight bid-ask spread of ⅛ point. This ideal spread, however, may increase as he gains more experience. "It's hard to minimize losses for stocks that have wide bid-asks because a stock could move 2 or 3 points quickly," says Hernandez. "But the more experienced you get, the more you can trade stocks with a wide spread, because if a stock starts moving against you, you can recognize that and be the first to get out."

Usually, Hernandez says, he does not follow a strict entry-point–stop-loss–exit-target trading plan. Most of the time he keeps a strict stop-loss of ½ point. Every now and then, however, he likes to go into a trade with a pair of mental stop-loss options—one set at ½ point and another at a more conservative ¼ point. "Sometimes the S&P will be rallying, the Nasdaq futures market is rallying, and my stock will be going down. In that situation, if the . . . [stock] is ¼ point against me, I'm going to hold it. But if it goes to ½ point, I'm going to get out—even though everything else looks positive," he says. "I'll get out, and if . . . [the stock] starts to turn [upward], I'll get back in."

Not surprisingly, Hernandez employs a similar strategy for winning trades. Usually, he says, he starts to "scale out" of a position after he's made ½ point. "I might buy 1000 shares of a stock, and if it rallies ½ point, I'll start scaling out. I'll get rid of 300 shares. And if it rallies another ¼ point, I'll get rid of another 300 shares. And then I'll leave the balance and let it go as far as the momentum will take it," he says. From time to time, Hernandez adds, he scales out earlier than at ½ point. "If I feel the momentum is switching, I might start scaling out after I've made ⅛ point," he says.

Beyond adhering to mental stops on losing trades and trailing stops on winning positions, there is one other golden rule that Hernandez follows: Never "double down" on a losing trade. "If a trade is going against me, I won't double it up," he says, emphasizing that this is a particularly important rule for a momentum trader.

When he wants to try an alternative strategy to momentum trading, Hernandez occasionally singles out stocks in a specific sector and trades them based on how they are performing in comparison with each other—a tactic known as *position trading*. "Sometimes, I'll look at the biggest stock in a particular sector and use it as my guideline to trade other stocks in that sector," he says. "I'll try to follow leading stock in sectors that are doing well or very poorly. For example, if biotechs are getting hammered, I might try to short them based on where the lead stock is going." This strategy can prove particularly beneficial, he says, when there is no momentum in the market.

The Art of the Short Sell

Roughly half the time he trades, Hernandez takes his rules and applies them to a short-selling strategy. "The longer I trade, the faster I'm getting. And I find that when the Nasdaq market is down 200 points, I make more money than when it's up 200 points. But if you talk to a new trader, . . . [he or she] will tell you that it's easier to make money in an up market," he says.

The reason you do not see too many new players in the direct access community taking the short end of a trade, says Hernandez, is because that strategy requires rapid decision-making skills. "It's a little harder to get short, obviously, because of the uptick rule. So you've got to be quick," he says. "Anybody can get long on an up move, but when a stock is dumping, it's tough to get short."

Still, Hernandez insists that if you stick to your rules and have trading experience, it is easier to make profits in a bearish market. "You look for that next uptick, and if you're really quick, you can hit that bid. And then, if . . . [the stock] ticks up, you can sell it at any level," Hernandez rationalizes.

From a rules standpoint, in Hernandez's book, there is no difference between shorting and going long. "It's exactly the same," he says. "If I'm shorting a stock, and it rallies ½ point, I'm getting out." While acknowledging that short selling "theoretically" requires a trader to assume unlimited risk, Hernandez asserts that as long as you stick by your rules, shorting is truly no more risky than going long. "When I'm shorting, I'm just analyzing the momentum in a stock that's weak, . . . and if you short a stock at $100, I think you'll be able to do something before it goes to $200," he says facetiously.

One method Hernandez uses to identify short-selling opportunities is to select one weak stock and one strong stock to keep an eye on, prior to the start of trading on any given day. "I try to find two stocks that I am familiar with. . . . And when the market starts to go negative, I'll . . . [locate] my weak stock and try to short it. And when the market is rallying, I will be trading the strong stock," Hernandez explains.

Execution Options

Regardless of whether he is selling short or going long, Hernandez says that he typically determines where to route an order by scanning best bid and offer data on his level II window. "If Island is on the offer, I'll just send an order directly to that ECN. If a market maker is on the offer, I'll send an order through SelectNet Preference," he says.

When he is "getting into a position," Hernandez says that he uses SelectNet 70 percent of the time. However, when he wants to exit a position, he relies primarily on direct ECN access. "When I'm getting out, I'm usually getting out on the offer, through Island," he says.

Hernandez says that his preference is to route orders directly to Island because that ECN offers the quickest executions. Unfortunately, he says, market makers are on the best bid or offer more frequently than Island. "The market makers are always on the offer somewhere," he says. "So, if a market maker is on the offer, I'm just going to take that through SelectNet. It could be Morgan Stanley one day or Goldman Sachs the next. It's not the same . . . [market maker], but somebody is always there."

One of the keys to success, Hernandez says, is getting to know the market makers who buy and sell the stocks you are interested in. Through experience, says Hernandez, you will eventually figure out which market makers actually move a specific stock. Eventually, he says, you will discover that some market makers play a significant role in affecting the price swings of specific stocks every day.

Moreover, there are also some market makers who are not always in the mix but emerge as the big buyer of a stock over a 1- or 2-week period. And once you identify that buyer, says Hernandez, you should be able to take advantage of your knowledge. "That whole week you're concentrating on that market maker so that any time he [or she] gets on that bid, you're jumping in front of him [or her] and lifting that offer," he says.

Over the course of time, adds Hernandez, you will get to learn which market makers will give you complete fills and which ones are just messing with your head. "Sometimes I don't even bother preferencing some of these market makers because they don't honor you," he says. "But eventually you get to learn who is really there [at their displayed price and size] and who is really not there, and then you know who to preference, via SelectNet, in crunch time." In the end, concludes Hernandez, the smart trader will stay with "whichever market makers have delivered the most consistent fills in the past via SelectNet."

Like every other direct access trader, when Hernandez decides he wants to route an order to a market maker, he has two SelectNet options to choose from: Preference, which sends the order to a specific market maker, and Broadcast, which displays the order to the entire market making community. However, Hernandez almost never uses the Broadcast option. "When you use SelectNet [Broadcast], the order usually keeps going down until it finds a market maker who will honor you. So you could get filled away from the market. . . . And I like to know what price I'm sending my order out to," he explains.

Hernandez usually places a market order to open a position and a limit order to close a position. Sometimes, he says, he will place a limit order to buy a stock on a pullback. Unlike some of his direct access brethren, however, Hernandez does not think that it is wise to use limit orders all the time. "When a stock is moving, I never use a limit order [to get in] because you'll never get it. Everybody's lifting stock, so it's almost worthless to put a [limit order] bid in," he says.

The Risk Factor

In terms of minimizing risk, Hernandez says that beyond staying true to your mental stop loss, the most effective step a trader can take is to create an effective money-management plan. To truly curb risk, he says, you have to be able to control your losses. And a good way to make sure you do that is to set maximum loss levels for yourself for any given day, week, and month. For example, depending on your trading capital, you might want to make up a rule that states that you cannot lose more than $500 in a day or $5000 in a week

However, although he has a maximum point level he is willing to lose per trade, Hernandez says that he does not have a standard maximum amount of money that he can lose on any given day or week. Rather, he says, the way he tries to protect against major losses is to take a break from his trading post when he is not executing well. "The first thing I'll do is step away for a few minutes and sit down and really focus on one good, winning trade," he says. "I get back to basics and just try and make sure that next trade is a winning trade."

One other tactic traders sometimes use to reduce risk is to keep multiple positions open. This strategy, which calls for a trader to spread his or her trading capital across a group of stocks, works well for a position trader, says Hernandez. "If you hedge it right, it does minimize your risk. For example, if you trade in the same sector and you feel [that] one stock is weak and one stock is strong, you can buy one and sell the other, . . . and I feel that kind of minimizes your risk," he says.

However, for momentum traders, Hernandez says that the "spread-out-your-trading-capital strategy" actually may increase your risk. In fact, Hernandez never keeps more than two positions open at once. "I personally like to stick to one or two stocks because I feel I'm more focused. I can't concentrate on three different stocks at the same time. I like to look for that moment where the momentum switches in a stock, and that's tough to do when you've got three or four [open] positions," he says. "You can't concentrate, obviously, 100 percent on a stock and get that exact moment where you see that . . . [trader] who's been bidding a stock up go off the bid, and then, boom, he's on the offer."

This moment, Hernandez explains further, is especially significant to a momentum trader because this is the point "where everybody is going to start hitting their bids to get out of their longs." If you are trading too many stocks, he says, you could miss that all-important moment. "Things change quickly, and if you miss your opportunity, then you are in trouble. . . . In half a second, a stock could move ½ point," says Hernandez.

Getting out of longs can be a tricky and risky proposition—particularly if you are trying to get rid of a stock that you believe is caught in a downward cycle. Indeed, if you need an example, all you have to do is look at Hernandez's worst single day as a direct access trader. On that day, he says, he lost $2000—primarily because he was desperately trying to close out a position on a stock he considered a dog.

"That day, I was long 500 shares of a stock that was coming off. And what I did was preference like six different people trying to get out. I preferenced each of them for my closeout position, which was 500 shares. And they all [honored] me," he says. "Usually, if you preference two or three . . . [people], you'll get 100 shares here and 200 there—especially when the stock is going down. . . . But I preferenced six . . . [people] for 500 shares, got [all the orders] honored, and wound up [in the hole] for 2500 shares."

The lesson here, of course, is to be careful not to let your desire to dump a stock override your strategy for exiting a position. For Hernandez, however, closing out all his positions during the course of the day is important because he does not like to hold stocks after the close.

Totally separate from his short-term account, Hernandez has a portfolio of long-term holdings. Since he holds multiple stocks in that account on a long-term basis, Hernandez says that he rarely, if ever, feels the need to keep a position open after the close "Anytime I want to hold overnight, I'll put a stock in my long-term account," he says.

One popular overnight strategy employed by some direct access traders is to only hold stocks that achieve their high at the close. However, Hernandez says that unlike in the past, stocks that achieve their high of the day at the close are no longer a lock to open higher the next morning.

"In the past, it was a rule that a stock that closed at its high was going to open up . . . [at a higher price] the next morning. But now, with all the . . . [market] volatility, I don't think that rule holds like it used to," says Hernandez. "I've seen stocks close on their high, and the next day they're down $20. . . . So I try to avoid taking home overnight as much as I can."

Thanks in part to his distaste for trading overnight, Hernandez says that he feels perfectly comfortable trading on margin. The only time anyone borrowing money to trade should think about adjusting their risk-management strategy, says Hernandez, is if they hold stocks after the close. Intraday margin trading, he says, is not any riskier than marginless trading. Moreover, he says that he is all for the proposal now sitting in front of the SEC that calls for direct access traders' maximum margin level for NYSE and Nasdaq stocks to be raised from 2:1 to 4:1. "I think it's only beneficial if you can put $1000 up and trade $4000 worth of stock," he says.

The Trading Day

Typically, before he officially begins his workday, Hernandez goes to the gym for a short workout. While he is at the gym, which is located in the same building as his office, Hernandez tunes into some early financial news from CNBC and CNN. Simultaneous with his workout, he says, he glances up at those financial channels "to get a feel for what sectors are weak and what sectors are strong for the day."

Right after his visit to the gym, Hernandez heads straight up to his office, usually arriving around 9 A.M. At that time, he checks out how stocks are performing in the premarket prior to the open. "Sometimes you get a pretty good idea about which direction the stock is moving in. You'll see the market makers trying to buy a stock, for example, in the pre open, and you kind of get a good feeling that this stock is going to be bid up today," says Hernandez.

Occasionally, if he sees a stock that he really likes, Hernandez will post a bid in the premarket, hoping to get hit prior to the open. Noting that he never preferences a market maker during the premarket, Hernandez says that posting a bid during this time is a relatively low-risk proposition. "If I get hit, fine. If I don't, I'm not going to go crazy and chase the stock in the open," he explains.

In the half hour before the open, Hernandez attempts to find three or four stocks to focus on for that day. He selects these issues by scrutinizing a stock's price movement and size. After he has found the stocks he would like to trade, Hernandez logs into his Nasdaq level II window a minute or two before the open—his most active trading period of the day.

The very first thing that catches his attention at the open—when he is trying to make between ½ and 1 point—is a stock's volume. "That kind of tells me whether the stock is going to be busy," he says. Hernandez has no minimum volume requirements to trade a stock but says that he tries to gauge how well a stock is performing by comparing its volume with the volume of other stocks in its sector.

Just after eyeing the volume, Hernandez tries to quickly determine if a stock has any momentum. "It could be something as simple as all the bids piling up. . . . You might see Instinet bidding for 10,000 and Morgan Stanley biding for 500, and the offers look a little shady. . . . So, if the bids are looking solid, the offers are looking weak, and the [S&P] futures are rallying, I'm looking to get long in that stock," he says.

One tactic he uses to get long is to quietly jump the queue on the bid. "You can actually jump in front of the bid and hide it so that people don't know you're bidding ahead of them," he points out. An alternative strategy for getting long, says Hernandez, is to simply "lift the offer or join the bid."

Whether he jumps the queue on the bid side, he says, largely depends on whether there are multiple players jacking a stock's price up. "If a stock's moving up on serious volume, that tells me there are some big buyers in there, and I don't mind jumping in front of those . . . [people]. However, if it's one . . . [person] taking a few bids and moving the stock up, I don't feel comfortable jumping in front," he says.

Besides volume and bid and offer data, Hernandez also analyzes a stock's time and sales report (located to the right of the level II window) from time to time. "That tells me where the actual trades are taking place," he says. "When I look at that, I look for people to start taking stock away from the offer or through the bid. . . . If a stock's offered at 90⅛ and I see prints at 90¼, I know this stock is moving up because people are taking it through."

Periodically, Hernandez also glances at his Standard & Poor's Futures and Nasdaq Composite charts and looks up a stock's resistance and support levels. Generally speaking, he likes to look up a stock's resistance and support data during the morning hours so that he can see where a stock has been over the last 2 days or week or month. "I'll kind of keep that [data] in the back of my head and use that in connection with my momentum trading," says Hernandez.

For example, he says, if he sees that a stock has rebounded after dropping below $100 on three separate occasions, he probably will attempt to short it. "I'll keep that in mind when I'm trading, and if the stock is dumping and going . . . [beneath] $100, I'm getting short because it's already bounced off three times," he says.

Throughout the course of the day, in fact, Hernandez is scanning the market for stocks in the $100 range. "When a stock gets near $100, I like to buy . . . [because] it usually breaks through that barrier for a few points. So I try to buy it as it is approaching $100," he explains. "It's a psychological thing. If the stock doesn't break $100, it has a tendency to go down."

At the close, through his direct access system, Hernandez prints out a report that tells him how much money he made or lost for each individual stock he traded. By analyzing the data, he says, he can really determine the types of stocks he should be trading. "At end of day, I'll go back and look at my notes. If I see that I'm losing money trading specific stocks every day, I'll stop trading them," Hernandez says.

After Hours Trading and Decimalization

Following the close, Hernandez—like most traders using direct access systems—has the opportunity to trade in the after hours market. However, noting that market makers are not required to honor orders after the close, he says that he rarely tries the after hours market.

"Today, the only reason I would trade after hours is if I'm stuck with a position and I'm trying to get out," says Hernandez.

The truth, Hernandez says, is that there is a "good chance" you are going to get stuck with a trade overnight if you enter a position after the close. "Basically, nobody adheres to any rules after hours. If you preference somebody, they don't have to honor you. So it's pretty much pot luck," he opines.

Nasdaq's upcoming conversion from fractions to decimals, in contrast to after hours trading, should provide some benefits to direct access traders, says Hernandez. Although Nasdaq is not scheduled to go live with decimalization for its first group of stocks until March, Hernandez says that through his Watcher-supplied direct access system, he can trade in decimals right now. Essentially, the big advantage that decimals offer Hernandez over traders who are still quoting in fractions is the ability to jump to the front of the queue.

For example, he says, if the best bid for a stock were 98¼ and you put in a bid of 98.2510, you could effectively jump ahead of the person trading in fractions—without that individual knowing it. "For the . . . [person] who . . . [puts in a] 98¼ bid for 10,000 shares, it looks like somebody's joined his bid when the 98.2510 bid is entered. But in fact, I just jumped in front of him," says Hernandez.

Still, though decimalization should produce some positive results for direct access traders, it also will present a few obstacles. For example, says Hernandez, the jump to decimals is expected to produce narrower spreads, and if spreads become smaller, then the profit a trader takes home per trade will be less. Therefore, he says, to generate the types of profits they yearn for, traders likely will have to trade more frequently in a decimalized environment.

Whether he or she is trading in decimals or fractions, to consistently generate profits, a direct access trader must set goals that outline how much he or she is willing to lose versus the profit he or she is looking to make—on a daily, weekly, and monthly basis, says Hernandez. The amount of money you are willing to risk should depend, he says, on your strategy and the amount of money you have to play with. However, he emphasizes that it is very important for each and every new participant in the direct access market to "expect to lose money" during the first 6 months.

When you start out, he says, it is also wise to trade in smaller share increments. A good size to start with, says Hernandez, is 100 shares per trade. "The general rule is to trade as small as you can when you start," he says.

Finally, Hernandez says, the inexperienced direct access trader should work hard to find some "second tier" stocks to trade. It all comes back to the experience factor, he says, and you will be out of your league if you attempt to buy or sell any of the market's "high-flying stocks." Hernandez says that these stocks, which sometimes move 30 or 40 points in a single day, are the playground of the trading elite—and therefore should be considered off-limits. "You want to trade in the minor leagues," he advises. "If you go into these A grade stocks, you're dead, because you are trading against the best."

7

QUESTIONS AND ANSWERS

Throughout the course of each and every direct access trader's career, there comes a time when the trader must define who he or she is. Although there is no magic formula for arriving at this definition, all traders can at least begin to mold and shape their identities by answering a series of key questions.

To define your profit and loss parameters, for example, you must first figure out how much capital you are willing to risk and what steps you are going to take to cut losses off. Similarly, to find the trading strategy that is best suited to you, you must determine the average (and maximum) amount of time you would like to hold positions.

Obviously, the responses to such queries will vary from trader to trader. Once you find the answers, however, they will serve as building blocks, empowering you to define your trading criteria and objectives.

In this chapter we will probe direct access traders, day trading executives, and trading education gurus to determine answers to seven of the most frequently asked questions about direct access trading.

Q: What factors should I consider prior to deciding where I'm going to route my order?

Harvey Houtkin, chairman and chief executive officer of the day trading firm All-Tech Direct, says that one important factor you must consider before sending an order to your final execution destination is the size you are hoping to get filled at. "If you're only looking to buy 500 or 1000 shares, you can let the Small Order Execution System (SOES) just take the offering. But if you think that you might be able to buy [a stock] on the bid, then you have to learn how to bid for stocks, and the best [quotes] are on electronic communication networks (ECNs)," he says.

A direct access trader, says Houtkin, also should consider the direction in which a stock is moving and the direction of the overall market. Moreover, he says that if you are going to send an order to a market maker by way of SOES or SelectNet, then you must figure out "which dealers are the substantive" players in the stock you are trading.

Taking into account the various order-routing options that are available to a direct access trader, Houtkin adds, it is also very important to understand the ins and outs of whichever direct access system you are using. "For someone just to come in and get our system and take it home probably would be like giving them an automatic weapon and saying, 'Here, why don't you go out and shoot some cans,' " he says. This said, Houtkin believes that once a trader grows to understand the intricacies of his or her direct access system, it is always preferable for him or her to route orders directly to an ECN.

Scott Ignall, a former direct access trader who now works as a software development manager at Tradescape.com, concurs that ECNs are the best execution destinations for Nasdaq orders. Around 5 years ago, Ignall says, SOES was the preferred choice of active online traders—because market makers often were reflecting 1000 shares over the network and filling for that size.

But now, he says, ECNs are the only execution mechanisms you can really count on to get complete fills. "The beauty of the ECN is if . . . [a match for your order] is there, and you want it, you can have it. They don't show 1000 shares and you go to buy 1000 and they only give you 100. If they say they're selling 10,000 and you want to buy them, you can have them. . . . Market makers, on the other hand, can show 100 shares and possess 10,000," says Ignall, who worked full time as a direct access trader for 2 years before jumping to the software development side in 1999.

Ignall, like Houtkin, also believes that direct access traders should study the moves of market makers who make markets in the stocks they trade diligently. "Every stock has a different market maker playing it. Goldman's market maker trading Intel is not the same Goldman person who is trading Microsoft. Two different people trade these stocks every day . . . [so] you have to understand what the market maker is doing individually, not what Goldman is doing [as a firm]," he says.

If you subscribe to a direct access system and simply watch the moves of market makers on level II for "2 weeks to a month" without making any trades, you can learn something, says Ignall. But Ignall—who traded an average of between 50,000 and 100,000 trades a day during his stint as a direct access trader—also says that on-the-job training is the only way you can gain intimate knowledge about the moves of specific market makers. Whichever way you choose to approach it, he adds, "reading what a market maker is doing and being able to react appropriately" are the most difficult things you will have to learn as a direct access trader.

Of course, if you try to avoid routing to market makers altogether—like direct access trader Pete Sweeney—reading their exact moves becomes less of a priority. Too often, Sweeney says, an order that is received by a market maker results in one thing he cannot tolerate—partial fills. "I have three or four basic trading strategies—one of which is to chase momentum. And with that strategy, partial fills are just the bane of my existence . . . because by the time the . . . [partial fill] comes back [to me] and I reroute my order, the [best] price is gone," explains Sweeney.

Currently, Sweeney routes most of his orders directly to the Archipelago ECN. Archipelago, he says, offers one value-added feature—the ability to reroute his order to another execution destination if it cannot find a match in its internal engine. However, generally speaking, Sweeney says that a trader should use the "consistency of fills" a specific ECN provides as the main criterion for determining which ECN he or she should route an order to.

Like Sweeney, John Bunda thinks that direct access traders should only use SelectNet or SOES if no other options are available. "They can take a long time to execute your orders, and they limit your ability to cancel orders," says Bunda, the chief technology officer of ProTrader

Technologies, the software development arm of ProTrader Group, an Austin, Texas–based day trading firm. "So the last place you want to go, really, is a Nasdaq system."

What is more, Bunda—who worked as a direct access trader for a year prior to assuming his current position—is not sure that SuperSOES will cure all the ills that plague Nasdaq's incumbent systems. One of the big question marks with SuperSOES, he says, is whether it will just inherit the problems that have plagued SelectNet. If this proves to be the case, he says, SuperSOES may not gain the trust of direct access traders because there would be too much doubt about the network's ability to process heavy order flow. "A lot of the . . . [the potential success] of SuperSOES depends on whether you will actually be able to get filled. . . . If you end up taking a half point slippage every time you use it, it is not going to be attractive to people," says Bunda.

ECNs, Bunda says, have a distinct advantage over both SelectNet and SOES in critical areas, such as speed and cost. "The day traders all love Island because it's fast and quick. The other ECNs are another tier down because they're a little slower and might cost a little more," he says.

When routing an order directly to an ECN, Bunda says that you should consider not only which of the ECNs has the best price but also which network is going to provide you with the fastest, most reliable fills. "For instance, you may not want to trade on Instinet because your broker charges you more for an Instinet trade than for an Island trade. . . . But if Instinet is out there bidding, and you're trying to get out, it might be better to take the more experienced Instinet fill than to try and offer it out on Island. Because as soon as the Instinet bid is gone, you might give up another price level."

Q: Do I need to maintain a stop loss for every order I enter, and should I use a mental stop or an automatic stop?

Peter Sweeney, a direct access trader who engages primarily in swing trading, says that he uses a mental stop for every order he enters. However, if he is going to trade intraday, he will sometimes use his direct access system to "mock up" electronic tickets—complete with stops—for specific stocks.

"This would require me to plug in, for example, sell x shares at x price and load it in [my system's] memory. So, in this situation, all I have to do is hit send, and then I'm out of the position," he says. "The only difference between this and an automatic [stop loss] is that I just have to make the decision to exit the trade."

ProTrader's Bunda says that regardless of whether you choose the mental or automatic route, you must have a stop loss, and you must adhere to it. "If you say I'm going to risk ½ point on a trade and it goes to ¾ before you get a chance to get out, don't hesitate and hope that maybe it will come back to that half," he advises.

Even if it means that you have to rely on your direct access system to execute automatic stops, Bunda says, you absolutely must have "complete discipline" when a stock hits your stop-loss level.

However, Bunda concedes that he prefers to use mental stops because they allow him to "manage a trade" on his own behalf. "As a human being, I can almost always do better than some sort of machine . . . because I can take so many more things into account as I'm executing the trade," he says.

While asserting that the stop loss is a vital tool that all direct access traders should use, Ignall—like Bunda—is not a big fan of the automatic stop. "What the automatic stop loss does for you is give you the ability to walk away . . . knowing that your risk is limited to a certain price level," he says. "But the automated feature . . . is a luxury that's not needed if you're sitting at your trading screen and have the ability to make up your mind quickly."

Generally speaking, he says, direct access traders have the ability to make rapid decisions and therefore can handle the responsibilities that come with using a mental stop. "Setting a mental stop loss is a little better for direct access traders because they know where their stop is, and then once . . . [the stock] reaches that level, they can just automatically sell it if they want to. But if they see some strength they have been waiting for, they can wait [to exit their position]," explains Ignall.

Q: What steps do I need to take to minimize my risk?

ProTrader's Bunda says that the best way to reduce risk is to "stay the course" with whichever strategy you employ. And a big part of staying the course, he says, is to exit a losing position as quickly as possible. "For me personally as a trader, the hardest part was when a loss got larger than my risk-management strategy permitted. . . . [I had] a tendency to hold on and hope that the stock will come back, [so that I could] . . . execute within the parameters of [my] strategy. But my experience is that

that was almost never a good way to approach it. . . . If the loss gets bigger, you should pull the plug," he says.

All-Tech's Houtkin agrees, noting that one of the most effective ways to minimize risk is simply to take your loss. "Just do it. . . . Get off your backside. Stop praying, stop wishing, stop hoping, and do what you know you're supposed to do," Houtkin advises. "Just take the action. I learned a long time ago [that] no action is an action [in the direct access trading world] because if you take no action, you've [effectively] chosen to hold a stock."

However, while you need to adhere to your stop loss, Houtkin says that it is important not to radically divert from your trading plan when you run into a string of consecutive losses. "A lot of people, when they lose a few times, they start pressing. . . . They force themselves into trades, doing things that they really shouldn't be doing. . . . They're trading out of panic because they want to get their money back. But that's the worst thing you can do," he says.

Meanwhile, Tradescape's Ignall says that one other important step a direct access trader should take to minimize risk is to learn everything about the system he or she is using—because having intimate knowledge of the system will allow them to "think in pressure situations and react correctly." Psychologically speaking, he says, it is also important to steer clear of any emotional attachment to a stock. "Remember that a stock is just four letters. It doesn't owe you anything when you lose money in it," Ignall says.

Just as important, he says, you should reevaluate your risk-reward ratio with every position you take, making sure that your potential gains are larger than your potential risk. "The gain should always outweigh the risk. That way, the odds are in your favor," says Ignall.

Q: Should I maintain long-term positions to counterbalance my short-term account?

A direct access trader's short-term account and long-term holdings should have "no relationship to each other," says Howard Abell, a trading guru who is the cofounder of the online trading education site invest2know.com. Abell says that it is natural for a trader to have both an earnings strategy (via short-term trading) and an investment strategy (via long-term positions) but emphasizes that the two strategies should not serve cross-purposes. "Active trading is an earning experience. It's like earning money day to day, going out and working. Long-term positions are more of an investment attitude—more passive. I separate the two," he says.

Keeping one's short- and long-term accounts separate, Abell says, is of paramount importance because long-term positions should never interfere with one's short-term view. "If people have long-term positions in stocks, that says to me that they don't really look at them. They have a long view of a year or two. . . . But what if they're looking at the daily fluctuations of those same stocks?" Abell asks rhetorically. "Then, emotionally, they're going to be colored in their perception of the vehicles they are trading."

However, in terms of short selling, Abell concedes that short-term traders occasionally can use their long-term positions to their advantage—because if you are shorting a stock you own, you do not have to borrow shares from the clearing firm. "If you're looking to use a long-term position as a trading vehicle [for short selling], it eliminates the necessity . . . [to adhere] to the uptick rule. . . . The uptick rule is waived because you own the stock," says Abell.

Indeed, "long-term positions give a trader the ability to sell into the market instantly," says Ken Johnson, CEO of the online trading education firm sixthmarket.com. "If I'm a very active trader and I own 5000 shares of Dell, I now have the ability to get the effect of a short sell any time I want by selling and buying it back," he says.

Noting that the "overwhelming majority of short-term traders are also long-term investors," Johnson says that one reason direct access traders swing both ways is simply because they have a good amount of "investable" capital. "Whether they have a million dollars holding Dell or a million dollars in cash, they can trade against both," he says.

However, Johnson also warns that since a trader's long-term account is really aimed at such things as "retirement and putting your kids through college," you should really attempt to keep short- and long-term holdings as separate as possible. "That [long-term account] is your nest egg, [so] you don't want to fool with that too much. You certainly don't want to put it at great risk, and you're not looking for as great a return there," Johnson advises.

Unquestionably, some direct access traders believe that their short- and long-term accounts should be maintained completely separate, like church and state in America. Don Merz, for example, says that his two accounts have "nothing to do" with each other. Through investments he's made in companies such as Microsoft, General Electric, and Pfizer, Merz says that his long-term account is now up between "35 and 40 percent." However, he relies on his direct access account as his primary money-making tool. "My long-term account is for retirement purposes. . . . My direct access account kicks . . . [butt]," Merz explains.

Chris Cropley, however, says that a direct access trader's short-term account can indeed get intertwined with long-term positions—at least on occasion. When you are trading via your direct access systems, he says, you sometimes stumble across "bargain" prices for stocks that have excellent long-term potential. And when this happens, Cropley says, it would be foolish not to snatch up those bargains and store them away for a while. "Sometimes you can see a stock like GE just take a nosedive in the middle of the afternoon, just because the Dow has dropped or whatever. And it's silly not to take advantage of that," says Cropley, a direct access trader who executes between 12 and 24 trades per day.

All-Tech's Houtkin, meanwhile, says that a direct access trader should hold long-term positions only if he or she "truly, consciously believes" there is a reason to do so. "You know what they say the definition of an investment is? A trade that went bad," he says with a chuckle.

Q: Under what circumstances should I hold a trade overnight?

In terms of evaluating whether you should keep a position open after the close, Houtkin says that the most important thing to remember is not to hold onto a stock simply because you have lost money on it. "If you're just holding it because it went down a quarter and you really don't want to take a quarter loss today, and you think it will be better tomorrow, then you're making a big mistake," cautions Houtkin.

When pondering whether you should hold a position overnight, he says, you should take a neutral approach and ask yourself, "If I didn't own the stock, would I be buying it right now?" Of course, there may be situations where the answer to this question will be "yes." For example, says Houtkin, if a stock is "running up" and breaking through a new high toward the market close, this may be sufficient reason to hold on to that stock—because stocks that finish strong have a tendency to open strong the next morning.

Similarly, ProTrader's Bunda believes that if a stock closes strongly, it makes sense to hold it overnight—because you can get out after the stock gaps up in the morning. However, he emphasizes that you have got to have a legitimate reason to hold the position after the close. "A lot of people will hold onto their losers overnight in the hope that they'll rise the next day. But that's dumb because it's not part of an overall strategy," he says. "This comes down to, again, your discipline in your approach to trading. If you have a strategy that says I'm going to hold something for 3 days, that's different from saying, 'I got into Dell and it got away from me . . . so I'm going to hold it overnight and hope it comes back.' . . . That's just stupid."

Tradescape's Ignall, in contrast, is not a fan of traders holding positions after the close under any circumstances. The markets following the close and prior to the opening, he says, are very illiquid, and there are not "many vehicles for getting in and out of stocks" quickly. Therefore, Ignall says, if you are long in a stock and happen to be down 5 points, you will have very limited opportunities to dump that position. "There is not a lot of liquidity before the market opens, . . . [so] if your stock is going up, you'll make a lot of money. And if it is going down, you'll lose a lot," he says.

Moreover, Ignall says that since active direct access traders have their "hands in a lot of different stocks," they may not have the "fundamental knowledge" of stocks that, say, a professional trader who is trading after the close may have. Lastly, he says, holding a position after the close takes away a direct access trader's speed advantage. "For an active trader, speed is essential. Your advantage is the speed at which you can think and the speed at which your software moves. . . . [But] when you trade overnight, trading . . . [becomes] more of a long-term game."

Q: Should I keep a daily journal of my trading activities?

Cropley says that he prints out a summary of his trading activity at the end of each trading day, courtesy of his CyBerCorp-supplied direct access system. This end-of-day printout supplies a history of the intraday trades Cropley has made, giving him the power to see what he did right and what false steps he took. And for Cropley, at least, this is extremely valuable information. "Going over . . . [your trading summary] every day, you can start to see when your system falls apart," says Cropley. "That's important because you have to consistently put together a new [trading] system and then trade it until it doesn't work any more."

Paul Hindes, president of the direct access trading systems firm Watcher Technologies LLC, agrees that traders who maintain a daily journal can "learn from their mistakes" and get better faster. "There is a reason that you have to be a human to do this trading. This is not program trading," he notes.

ProTrader's Bunda also thinks that keeping a daily trading journal is a good idea. Personally, Bunda says, keeping a daily trading journal did not push him to great heights as a direct access trader—but that was partly because he just "didn't like the paperwork" that the practice required.

If you are assiduous about keeping a diary, he says, you will learn what you did right and wrong over the course of a day. In turn, he says, you will develop the "survival skills" you need to "stay away from the bad trades" on a regular basis.

What is more, by enabling you to work out the kinks in your trading strategy, a trading journal can help you keep your emotions in check, says Bunda. And by taking emotion out of your trading equation, you should be able to trade more effectively. "Direct access trading is not as sexy as a lot of people think it is. People think they're going to make a fortune on the latest dot-com stock or whatever. But if you want to, over time, be a successful trader, you have to pick a strategy and execute it," says Bunda. "So I think that for someone who is going to actually figure out the game and become a successful trader, . . . [keeping a daily trading journal] is important."

By maintaining a daily journal, echoes Tradescape's Ignall, a trader can expose his or her strengths and weaknesses. For example, he says, the journal should highlight whether your style is better suited to a buy-low, sell-high strategy versus a short and cover strategy.

Moreover, Ignall says, keeping a daily journal allows you to "study your habits" in a calm environment, after the chaos of the trading day has passed. This emotionless environment, he says, should help you evaluate your trading decisions more objectively.

However, this said, Ignall also emphasizes that the daily trading journal is really a tool designed for the beginner to intermediate-level direct access trader. "For the advanced trader, who has done a lot of trading, you can assume that their psyche and their decision-making level have advanced beyond evaluating every trade," he says.

For traders who choose to keep a journal, the technology to do so is, for the most part, already in place. Most direct access systems, says Houtkin, already have integrated position-keeping software into their network so that a trader can keep track of a stock on a day-by-day, minute-by-minute, or second-by-second basis. "This type of technology is built right into the system. . . . You could get a copy of every trade you make, every order you put in, and every order you canceled . . . [right] on your screen," he says.

Q: During what periods of the trading day can I make/lose the most money?

Bunda says that without question the highest-risk/highest-reward periods of the trading day are the open and the close. In terms of risk, he says, the open represents the greatest potential danger because that is when the largest price movements occur. "That is when you have the most liquidity, most activity, and the volatility is the greatest," he says.

Tradescape's Ignall concurs that the open is the most risky period of the day for direct access traders. During the first half hour or hour of trading, he says, stocks tend to move quickly in a certain direction. And if you take a position on the opposite side of that direction, you are definitely in trouble. "The stocks move where they are going to move. And if you're in the way, they'll roll right past you," he says.

However, while agreeing that the open has the "most volume" and the "most volatility," All-Tech's Houtkin says that depending on your specific strategy, volatility and huge price swings may be right up your alley. "If you're just basically doing de facto market making, you might prefer more stable, quiet times, where you can buy and sell and use the spread as your friend," he says. "On the other hand, if you're looking for momentum moves, you probably will get more of them in the opening, . . . [when] stocks are gapping up or gapping down, and you might want to sell into them or buy into them."

DECIMALIZATION AND AFTER HOURS TRADING: PEERING INTO THE FUTURE

In today's world, when we think of a direct access trader, we probably get a visual of a fast-thinking gunslinger who buys and sells stocks on an intraday basis in small, fractional price increments. In the very near future, however, we will have to alter this mental portrait.

As we write this book, the major U.S. stock markets are either knee-deep or neck-deep in decimalization projects that will change the quote increment for all stocks from fractions to decimals. Moreover, with shorter settlement dates, straight-through processing (STP), and global linkages to international stock markets on the horizon, 24-hour trading is slowly working its way into the American mind-set.

Currently, the after hours trading market in the United States is too illiquid and risky to attract a sizable pool of direct access traders. However, as cross-border trading becomes more accessible and safer, after hours is likely to become a more popular venue to trade in. Later on in this chapter we take a closer look at the present and future of the postclose trading environment. Right now, however, we are going to focus in on decimalization.

On August 28, 2000, when they converted a combined 13 stocks from fractions to decimals, the New York Stock Exchange (NYSE) and the American Stock Exchange (Amex) jumpstarted the U.S. securities industry's historic migration to a new quotation structure. Of course, this was just phase 1. Around 1 month later, phase 2 kicked in, when the pair of primary markets morphed another 100 stocks into decimals.

To measure the impact these initial two decimalization phases had on stocks, Dr. Robert Wood—a professor of finance at the University of Memphis's Fogelman College of Business and Finance—and Sugato Chakravarty—a professor at Purdue University—performed two separate studies. The first study tracked the activity of phase 1 stocks for a period of 15 days prior to the decimal conversion and 10 days after the switch. The second study tracked the activity of phase 2 stocks from August 28 to September 22 (before decimalization) and from September 25 through October 6 (after decimalization).

Although the results of these two studies were not exactly alike, they were similar enough to reveal some interesting trends. For example, the studies collectively showed that as a result of decimalization, spreads narrowed, the bid-ask depth decreased, and the price increments for stocks dwindled. Moreover, the studies showed that regional exchanges that traded the decimalized stocks were at the best bid and offer more frequently than either NYSE or Amex—and also experienced more daily quote changes than the primary markets.

Undeniably, one of the most significant—and expected—conclusions of the studies was that after decimalization the spreads for both Amex and NYSE stocks tightened significantly. In phase 1, Amex stocks narrowed by 47 percent, whereas NYSE stocks tightened by 38 percent.[1] In phase 2 there was a slight dropoff in the degree of tightening, but the effective spreads for the five Amex and five NYSE stocks tracked by the study still narrowed by 31 and 22 percent, respectively.[2]

Wood says that the primary reason that spreads narrowed is that, thanks to the smaller tick size for stocks, traders can now "jump the queue" easier than ever before. In other words, now that stocks are being traded in reduced price increments, traders are more inclined to place an order that elevates them to best bid or offer status. "The hurdle to post a new quote is much smaller, and what that means is you get a tighter spread," says Wood. "For small investors, that's really good news, because they're going to be able to trade at lower costs."

However, while narrower spreads may lead to cheaper trading costs, they also tend to be accompanied by a decline in the total number of bid or offer orders listed for a stock in that stock's limit-order book. In phase 2, the bid-ask depth for Amex stocks dropped 46 percent, whereas the depth of NYSE stocks decreased a whopping 63 percent.[3] These results support Wood's hypothesis that as the bid or offer gets closer to the "equilibrium price," the depth of the order book for a stock will decrease. "When the tick size gets smaller—which [produces] a reduction of trading costs and causes volume to go up—we [inevitably] see the amount that's offered on the bid and ask spread become smaller," he says.

Some industry observers argue that decreasing bid-ask depths will have a negative impact on liquidity. However, Wood says that the positive results of decimalization override the reduction of the order book size. "I don't think . . . [decreased bid-ask depths] will affect most small traders because they're not trading in big size. It's going to make it harder, in some sense, for institutional investors because they're going to have to work harder to obtain liquidity. But, nevertheless, they're able to obtain tighter spreads as they work to get that liquidity. So that's the tradeoff. . . . They're getting cheaper trading costs, but they have to work harder to get them," Woods explains.

Just as it had an impact on spreads and the bid-ask depths, decimalization also strongly influenced the increment sizes traders chose to buy and sell stocks in. With regard to phase 1 stocks, before decimalization, roughly 56 percent of best bid and offer quote changes for the Amex stocks occurred at sixteenths, whereas 38 percent occurred at eighths. After decimalization, 25 percent of the quote changes for those same stocks occurred at 1 cent, whereas 79 percent occurred at 5 cents or less. The NYSE stocks, meanwhile, experienced similar results. Prior to decimalization, 78 percent of quote changes in the NYSE stocks occurred at sixteenths, whereas 18 percent occurred at eighths. Following decimalization, 32 percent of the changes for NYSE stocks occurred at 1 cent, whereas 82 percent occurred at 5 cents or less.[4]

Noting that the phase 2 results[5] in this category were comparable with phase 1, Wood says that the quote increment changes provide clear evidence that traders are jumping the queue like never before. However, he says that it is too early to tell whether the 1 cent increment will emerge as the standard increment for decimalized stocks. "From what I hear, a lot of the market makers are experimenting. They don't really know how to trade yet exactly in a decimal world. Some of the more sophisticated ones . . . are developing algorithms that they are using to generate quotes," says Wood. "I think that we will see them go through an experimentation period and then settle into a quoting pattern. But it's a little hard to tell right now."

What was easy to decipher, based on the results of the studies, was that the regional markets now have more of a fighting chance to achieve best bid and offer (BBO) status for stocks listed on the NYSE and the Amex. During phase 1, regional markets experienced a much greater improvement of their BBO frequency than either the NYSE or the Amex. In fact, BBO frequency at regionals such as the Cincinnati Stock Exchange, the Pacific Exchange, and the Chicago Stock Exchange increased dramatically. In contrast, the Amex (−5.6 percent) and the NYSE (−10 percent) both experienced a decline in their frequency at the BBO.[6]

In phase 2, the disparity between the regionals' BBO frequency and the primary markets' BBO frequency was not as dramatic. However, regional markets—including the Cincinnati, Pacific, and Boston stock exchanges—still improved the amount of times they were at the BBO.[7]

Wood says that the disparity in BBO frequency is indicative of the fact that, thanks to decimalization, the cost of supplying liquidity has declined. "The regionals were never able to compete with the NYSE on price. And now it appears that suddenly they're able to compete on price because the tick increment is so much smaller," explains Wood.

What is more, in addition to enjoying more frequent BBO status, the regional markets that trade decimal-converted NYSE and Amex stocks experienced more daily quote updates than the primary markets. In phase 1, the number of quote updates performed by NYSE and Amex specialists remained steady. However, fueled by quote updates performed by the regional markets, the overall daily quote frequency of the Amex and NYSE stocks grew by 49 percent.[8]

Moreover, in phase 2, the daily quoting frequency of regional specialists trading Amex stocks increased anywhere from 27 to 121 percent (compared with an increase of between 45 and 87 percent for NYSE stocks). Meanwhile, during that same period, the daily quote frequency of Amex and NYSE specialists dropped 11 and 5 percent, respectively.[9] Overall, daily quoting frequency during phase 2 increased 24 percent.

This rise in quote updates, says Wood, simply reflects the fact that people can do a "much better job of jumping the queue now."

One anticipated result Wood did not find in his studies is an increase in volatility. After decimalization, he says, volatility in the stocks tracked by the studies remained relatively stable. "I had talked to a number of buy-side traders who claimed that they had experienced an increase in volatility. But when we looked at our data, we didn't see that," says Wood.

However, while the switch to decimals did not greatly affect volatility, it did have an impact on the size of orders being placed. In both studies, the share size for the stocks being scrutinized were divided into five classifications: small trades (500 shares and fewer), medium1 trades (500–999 shares), medium2 trades (1000–4999 shares), medium3 trades (5000–9999 shares), and large trades (10,000 shares or more).

In phase 1, there was not enough data for Wood to draw any conclusions about relative trade size. However, in phase 2, while the NYSE stocks remained relatively unchanged, the trade size for the Amex stocks took a turn toward the smaller end of the spectrum.[10]

Down the road, Wood says, decimalization should bring about an overall reduction in trade size. "I think we'll see an increase in smaller orders because we'll see smaller limit orders being posted, and people will be hitting those smaller limit orders," he says.

All in all, Wood says that the studies show that decimalization will yield considerable benefits—especially for the small individual investor. "I think instead that this decimalization stuff really favors the small trader, who is suddenly able to jump the queue," says Wood. "If you're the one who's doing it and you're a retail trader, that's a huge advantage, potentially, . . . [because] a lot of retail traders do not understand that you can buy at the bid. They have no idea about that."

WHAT OF NASDAQ STOCKS?

Wood's studies, as we have already mentioned, focused exclusively on listed stocks. However, while it is likely that decimalization will bring about reduced spreads in Nasdaq stocks (just as it has done in the listed markets), it is difficult to say with any certainty what other results the transition from fractions to decimals will yield in the Nasdaq market.

Nasdaq began its transition to decimals in March 2001. After Nasdaq completes its decimalization project, the stock market's minimum price variation (or quote increment) will drop all the way down to 1 cent. This fact alone could lead to tighter spreads, since most Nasdaq stocks today are traded in quote increments of $\frac{1}{16}$ (6.25 cents) or higher.

Honestly speaking, until Nasdaq is up and running with decimals for a few months, we will not know the true degree of change decimalization will bring. In the meantime, however, at least we can ponder a few important questions. For example, will decimalization ultimately yield reduced trading costs for investors? What are the pros and cons of the fraction-to-decimal transition for the direct access trader? And will decimalization favor any particular type of direct access trading strategy?

Paul Hindes, Watcher Technologies' president, says that it is too early to tell which strategies could flourish in a decimalized environment. However, he says that decimalization should lead to narrower spreads, larger volume, and most significantly, lower trading costs. "Higher volumes generally will mean a lower fee per transaction. So the average cost per transaction will likely go down," he theorizes.

On a more sour note, Hindes says that if you are a momentum trader, decimalization will force you to execute more trades to make the same amount of money you make today. Since the spreads will be narrower, he reasons, you will have to fight for smaller profits with each trade you make. Therefore, you will need to implement a more active trading plan and—just as important—choose a superior direct access system. "You will need a piece of software and a trading system that will be able to accommodate the increased volume and provide the speed and reliability necessary to take advantage of the short moves in stock prices," says Hindes. "If you don't have a system that's fast enough, that executes trades when you push the button, then you're not going to make those short moves. So it's going to become increasingly important for people who are momentum traders to have faster, more reliable systems."

However, some stock market participants believe that beyond forcing you to reevaluate your incumbent trading system, the switch to decimals should favor scalpers over other types of direct access traders. ProTrader Technologies' Jon Bunda says that if decimalization has its expected impact, we may see more traders trying to "sell at the offer and buy at the bid" in an effort to make the spread. "If liquidity is magically created by decimalization—meaning that you have narrower spreads and there is more stock for sale or to be bought—it's going to make it easier to control your risk. So any strategy that requires good risk management in that kind of a situation could benefit [from decimalization]. In contrast, it's going to be of less importance to somebody who is swing trading or playing bigger market moves," he says.

However, while asserting that narrower spreads would help a scalper control risk, Bunda says that the really important issue that needs to be addressed is whether the conversion to decimals will lead to more liquidity in Nasdaq stocks. Without liquidity, he says, it is hard to imagine that spreads in Nasdaq stocks will narrow materially. And Bunda, for one, does not see the conversion from fractions to decimals leading to enhanced liquidity. "Spreads are really a function of liquidity, and decimalization itself will not create liquidity," he says. "Liquidity is not a function of what the price is quoted in. It's a function of how many people are . . . [at that price] with stock to buy or sell. And narrowing spreads really has a lot more to do with the actual liquidity that's there rather than how the stock is priced."

Bunda believes that the primary reason we are seeing narrower spreads in NYSE and Amex stocks that have made the switch to decimals is because of the "novelty of decimalization." However, decimal trading should be less of a novelty for direct access traders who trade Nasdaq stocks. That group, says Bunda, has possessed the ability to trade in finer price increments (all the way up to $\frac{1}{256}$) for the last 2 years. And during that period, spreads on Nasdaq stocks have narrowed. "Remember, the capability [for the direct access trader] to narrow the spread is there today. You can jump in there $\frac{1}{32}$ above the bid or $\frac{1}{256}$ below the offer. That capability has been there with the ECNs for years," he says. "So, if liquidity increases, spreads will narrow, regardless of whether we quote prices in decimals or fractions."

Undoubtedly, liquidity will be a key factor to watch after decimalization of Nasdaq trading. Following the conversion to decimals, liquidity in Nasdaq stocks likely will remain stable—but it will be spread out through different price levels for each individual stock, says Bunda. In this scenario, he says, the total number of partial fills will rise, and consequently, the number of individual transactions that it takes a trader to "build a position of a given size" will increase.

"What could happen is that you'll end up having more split fills. So, if you're going to buy 1000 shares, you're going to get 100 at this price,

300 a penny higher, and 400 a nickel higher than that," says Bunda. "[So] your fills . . . [will be] split among several different orders rather than all filled at the same price on one ticket."

Moreover, Bunda says that if decimalization brings about more partial fills, the potential cost savings that could be derived from narrower spreads may be nullified. "Depending on how I'm executing those orders, . . . [split fills] may end up adding to my commission costs. . . . Hopefully, I'm making it up on the other side by getting better prices. But depending on how my broker bills me for those fills, my commission costs could go up," he says.

All in all, Bunda believes that decimalization could have a fairly significant psychological impact on the less active individual investor community—influencing the way they think about "what a round number is" and what price they should bid or offer a stock at. However, he does not think the switch to decimals will cause a big stir among direct access traders. "Over the long haul, I don't think . . . [decimalization] will really affect day traders or direct access traders at all, compared with the way things are right now," says Bunda.

However, James Lee says that the transition to decimals will be a "net benefit" for direct access traders. Lee, the president of the Electronic Traders Association (ETA)—an industry group representing day trading firms—does not think that decimalization will influence the trading patterns of direct access traders. However, he says that since decimalization is going to "incentivize" less sophisticated online traders to trade in finer increments, it should produce indirect benefits for direct access traders. "Coupled with the order-handling rules, this will create narrower spreads and more liquidity in and around those spreads as people are more active with their limit orders," says Lee, noting that direct access traders should be able to capitalize on these trends.

R.I.P. PFOF?

While it may be true that the conversion to decimals will not have a tremendous impact on direct access traders, it could significantly affect this group by eliminating—or greatly reducing—payment for order flow (PFOF). As we explained earlier in this book, PFOF is an arrangement in which an online brokerage firm routes a customer order to a market maker. The market maker, in return, pays the broker a small fee (usually a penny per share).

Today, this practice is still fairly common. However, Watcher Technologies' Hindes says that since spreads are likely to narrow after decimalization, market makers will have "less and less money to share" with online brokers in return for order flow. As a result, he says, the number of PFOF arrangements should decrease. However, since the trading infrastructure of some firms is built completely around PFOF arrangements, Hindes says that the total disintegration of such agreements is still a ways off.

Like Hindes, ProTrader's Bunda thinks that PFOF will become less palatable to market makers following the Nasdaq's jump to decimals. "If spreads do narrow in some material way, certainly that would squeeze the margins of the guys who are doing the payment for order flow. And it might reduce the amount they pay for order flow or even make the whole business . . . [untenable]," he says.

Down the road, says Bunda, it is likely that we will see more and more orders being routed directly to ECNs and/or SuperSOES. "If the spreads narrow, maybe the . . . [people] who are giving payment for order flow will decide it's not a profitable business for them anymore, and maybe they will tell E*TRADE that they're going to start paying less for order flow," he says. "But then, the . . . [online discount broker] might just turn around and say that instead of doing PFOF, we'll just execute those orders directly. Meaning, rather than [executing orders] indirectly through one of these market makers, they'll just dump them directly into SuperSOES or an ECN."

Currently, if an online broker routes an order to a market maker, the chances of that order being executed immediately are not great. The market maker, at his or her discretion, can hold the order and search for a better price. However, in the future, if online brokers decide to pass up market makers in favor of routing orders directly to SuperSOES or an ECN, that order stands a greater chance of getting executed immediately. And more orders being executed immediately translates into greater volatility for Nasdaq stocks, says Bunda. "If those orders just start flowing into the market, essentially what you'll get is more direct liquidity," he says. "So you could imagine that would create more volatility in a stock."

Weighing all the different factors that currently influence Nasdaq stock trading, Bunda says that it is likely that PFOF will soon come to an end. However, he says that the death of PFOF will come as a result of evolution rather than decimalization. "I believe that's going to happen, but . . . [it will have] nothing to do with decimalization. It's an economics issue. . . . There will come a point where having a human touch a lot of these orders will become unprofitable," he says.

ETA's Lee, meanwhile, thinks that all forms of "preferencing relationships," including PFOF and "internalization," will soon either be diminished or eliminated. The Securities and Exchange Commission (SEC), he says, has been concerned about these types of relationships and is now taking steps to do something about them.

Step one, he says, is to oversee additional securities industry's conversion to decimals. However, the SEC, says Lee, is also reviewing a set of "fair disclosure rules" that would force market participants to more clearly describe the process they go through to route orders. "I think that the disclosure rules that the SEC has pending, coupled with decimals, will work to eliminate or severely reduce this practice of preferencing," says Lee. "People are becoming increasingly knowledgeable, and they will not tolerate, if they are aware of it, this practice of selling order flow off to the highest bidder."

One group that potentially could benefit from the reduction or elimination of PFOF—aside from direct access traders—is the ECNs. Since they splashed onto the scene in 1997, ECNs have helped narrow spreads in Nasdaq stocks significantly. And with decimals threatening the logic behind PFOF agreements, ECNs may play an even bigger role in the future. "If you can't internalize order flow profitably, . . . you're not going to be in a position to pay a lot for order flow," says Kim Bang, president of the Bloomberg Tradebook ECN. "And if you can't pay for order flow, then the large online brokerage firms may start to . . . turn to superior execution solutions for their investors. And that will create a greater opportunity for ECNs to compete with market makers for that order flow."

In the end, the conversion to decimals should both yield benefits and present obstacles for direct access traders. Don Merz, a direct access trader, says that he is not certain whether decimalization is going to help or hurt him. However, he says that the bottom line is that the change is not necessary. "What are we going to be fighting for, pennies now?" Merz asks rhetorically. "One of the explanations being thrown around [for decimalization] is that investors don't understand fractions. But if you don't understand fractions, you shouldn't be in the game in the first place."

AFTER HOURS: THE SEARCH FOR LIQUIDITY

After hours trading, unlike decimal trading, has been around for a couple of years. However, just as it will influence the success or failure of decimalization, liquidity—or the lack of liquidity—will determine the future of the after hours market.

In comparison with 1 year ago, says Bunda, there are a lot more direct access traders participating in today's after hours market. However, there is still not enough liquidity in that market to attract a significant population of direct access traders. "It's one of those chicken and egg problems," Bunda says.

While asserting that there is no question that the United States is headed toward 24-hour trading of stocks, Hindes agrees. "The spreads are still too wide in the after hours market, even on fairly active stocks," he says.

This said, however, there are at least a few direct access traders who are testing their luck in the after hours market. And one of the most popular strategies that comes into play after hours, says Hindes, is news- or events-based trading. "Any sort of announcement after hours presents an opportunity to take a position and then close it at the open," he says.

Trading stocks based on news, Bunda concurs, is a favorite after hours strategy employed by direct access traders. However, he adds that "fading the conventional wisdom" was one other strategy he was fond of when he traded after hours during his direct access days.

With this strategy, Bunda explains, a trader might short stocks that get gapped up on news after hours—based on the hypothesis that there's a good chance those stocks will fall down a few pegs after the open. "The thing that has worked for me in the past is fading the trend. You basically figure if the stock is bid way up on good news or pounded way down on bad news, chances are, once the market opens and there is a lot of liquidity, you are going to regress toward the mean. So you play against those wild swings," he explains.

Meanwhile, direct access trader Peter Sweeney says that he is much more inclined to trade before the open than after the close. Trading just before the open is less risky than after hours trading, he says, because there is more liquidity in the market from 8 to 9:30 A.M. than there is from 4 to 6 P.M.

Buying and selling stocks in the premarket, Sweeney adds, can prove a particularly lucrative strategy during periods when the market is performing well. "I don't do it very often, . . . but during . . . [a recent] strong period in the market, you in essence could read the tape on CNBC and find out what stocks were really going to move that morning. And then you could jump on the momentum before the masses of the world had a chance to do it," he recalls.

RISKY BUSINESS

Truthfully, there is no foolproof strategy you can employ when you are trading after the close. It is a risky proposition, filled with the pitfalls that accompany buying and selling stocks in an illiquid—and often volatile—market.

All-Tech's Houtkin says that unless you have some very specific talents, you would be wise to avoid after hours trading. "A lot of the active stuff that goes on after hours is news-related, . . . [so] unless you have a real ability to analyze the news and figure out if it's good or bad, I say stay away from after hours trading," he says.

Thanks to the volatility, trading after hours is a particularly bad idea for inexperienced direct access traders, says Tradescape's Ignall. If you end up on the wrong side of a stock move after hours, says Ignall, you could be in serious trouble—because you may not be able to find somebody to bail you out before you have taken some serious losses. "Since there are fewer market players after the close, you can't be as active as you would be during normal business hours," Ignall explains.

Sixthmarket.com's Johnson, meanwhile, says that the lack of liquidity after hours makes that market a dangerous proposition for all direct access traders—not just the less experienced ones. "I basically encourage people right now not to trade after hours. It's just so thinly traded that I'm not sure you're looking at real quotes," he says.

Similarly, ProTrader's Bunda advises against trading after hours because there are few people participating in that market and a stock can move "huge amounts" based on very little activity. "I think if you're really actively trading pre- and postmarket, that's where you are the most exposed. That's where you're at the greatest risk because there is no liquidity," he says. "The market can dry up on you in no time, and you can have a really hard time trying to exit a position if you can't afford to hang in there."

Liquidity in the after hours market, he adds, is not going to "build slowly over time." However, he also says that if some market participants began to make markets in specific stocks after hours, the market could become much more liquid. "The market is wide open right now for anybody to come in and say, 'Hey, I want to be a market maker.' . . . The opportunity is there to kind of take the market away from the specialist, by being a specialist yourself. So far, we don't see anybody doing that, but the opportunity is clearly there," says Bunda.

However, the ETA's Lee—noting that direct access traders have had the ability to trade postclose (via connectivity to Island and Instinet) for years—says that U.S. stocks traded after hours today have almost no liquidity. "The bottom line is that there is not much of a market in after hours," he says. "Except for earnings releases and news events, there's not much trading going on."

At this point, says Lee, the only way the U.S. after hours market could generate the liquidity it so desperately needs is if Nasdaq goes live with more trading linkages to different international stock markets. Nasdaq, Lee notes, has already formed joint ventures with equity exchanges in Asia and is currently scanning the market to find a big exchange partner in Europe.

More direct access traders in the United States will trade after hours, Lee says, after Nasdaq goes live with trading interfaces to major stock markets in Europe and the Pacific Rim. Lee reasons that since trading "always follows the sun," the busiest, most liquid stock markets are going to be the ones that are positioned under the midday sun. Those are the markets, he says, which are going bring liquidity to the after hours market because they will be the ones in which direct access traders will be most interested in trading.

Eventually, says Lee, we will likely see a "24-hour trading day," where a direct access trader at a U.S. day trading office is going to be trading Nasdaq stocks at noon and European stocks at 4 A.M.

STP AND T+1

Before we see any real commitment to trading international equities after hours, we may first have to draw closer to the securities industry's goal of achieving *straight-through processing* (STP)—the complete front- to back-office automation of trades. In an STP world, a cross-border trade would get routed, matched, executed, and settled in a paper-free environment without any human intervention.

Achieving STP is important because, according to a study performed by the securities industry consulting firm TowerGroup, cross-border trades, as of July 2000, were failing at a clip of 20 percent. Thus, in order to provide U.S. traders with the confidence and comfort they need to trade international stocks more often, major strides toward achieving STP are going to have to be made. However, Hindes says that the good news is that when STP becomes a reality, it potentially could swing open a whole new door to liquidity in the after hours cross-border market. "STP is a cross-border initiative, so it will allow and facilitate cross-border trading with lower risk," he says.

To get to the point where traders feel comfortable trading around the clock, the U.S. securities industry is also going to have to shorten its settlement cycle for trades. Currently, trades are settled according to a *T+3 structure*—meaning that a trade must be settled no more than 3 days after it has been executed. The ultimate goal, however, says Hindes, is to achieve same-day trade settlement—or T+0. "We're going to have to go to T+0 to have real 24-hours-a-day trading," he says.

Hindes says that if we can get to the point where trades are settled on the same day, the risks associated with trading after hours would diminish significantly, and postclose trading therefore would become a more appealing option for direct access traders. However, he also cautions that any traders waiting for the settlement date to be shortened should not hold their breath.

Before we achieve T+0, we must first move to T+1—an event that is not scheduled to take place until 2002. And since shortening the settlement cycle is a process that requires getting every clearing firm on Wall Street on the same page, Hindes has serious doubts about whether the securities industry can meet its T+1 date. "The technological foundation of Wall Street has some very large stones in it. It's not made of some flexible material," he says. "So, though the official date for hitting T+1 is 2002, I don't believe that there is anyone on Wall Street who believes that we are going to make that date."

Beyond STP and T+1, one last issue that could affect direct access traders in the future is consolidation among ECNs. At this moment, some ECNs just do not have enough volume to sustain their existence. Therefore, says Hindes, it is logical to predict that some of the small ones will either die or be swallowed up by a larger ECN. "I can't see why the smallest ECNs will continue to exist. If there's no volume, there is no way they can continue to exist," he says.

Tradescape.com chairman Omar Amanat, in sharp contrast, sees no reason why ECNs not only can continue to thrive but also can actually grow. Amanat says that since market makers are "willing to commit and risk their own capital" on both sides of a trade, they will always have a place—as liquidity providers—in the Nasdaq market. However, he also says that there is "no question that ECNs currently offer a faster, smarter, better" way to trade.

"Right now, there are 600 market makers on the Nasdaq. They have capital risk, counterparty risk, [and an] immense amount of overhead. . . . ECNs, on the other hand, have a very fixed, minimal amount of overhead, and everything else is variable costs," he says. "So, if anything, I think ECNs might multiply and proliferate because the business model in and of itself makes so much sense."

NOTES

1. Sugato Chakravarty (www.sugato@purdue.edu) and Robert A. Wood (University of Memphis), The Effect of Decimal Trading on Market Liquidity, An Executive Summary of Phase 1, Table 5, p. 23.

2. Sugato Chakravarty (www.sugato@purdue.edu) and Robert A. Wood (University of Memphis), The Effect of Decimal Trading on Market Liquidity, An Executive Summary of Phase 2, Table 5.

3. Decimal Study 2, Table 6.

4. Decimal Study 1, Table 3, pp. 20 and 21.

5. Decimal Study 2, Table 3.

6. Decimal Study 1, Table 2, p. 19.

7. Decimal Study 2, Table 2.

8. Decimal Study 1, Table 1, pp. 17 and 18.

9. Decimal Study 2, Table 1.

10. Decimal Study 2, Table 8.

FINAL THOUGHTS

Throughout the course of this book we have explored the different strategies direct access traders use to maximize profits and minimize losses. Moreover, we have discussed, in depth, the underlying issues that drive the day-to-day business decisions of traders and have outlined the initiatives that could change the direct access landscape in the future.

Still, there are a few questions we have not answered, including

- How many direct access traders exist?
- How long is the learning curve for a new direct access trader?
- What percentage of direct access traders actually make money, and what percentage eventually quit the business?
- Will direct access technology eventually wind its way into the mainstream?

James Lee, president of the ETA, estimates that there are currently 10,000 direct access traders in the United States. Collectively, he says, these traders account for roughly 15 percent of the total dollar volume of the Nasdaq.

The learning curve for first-time direct access traders, Lee says, is roughly 6 months. However, he says that before exploring the issue of what percentage of traders makes money versus losing money, it is important to clarify the definition of a direct access trader. Direct access traders, Lee notes, are in total control of their order flow—using sophisticated technology to route orders directly to their preferred execution destinations.

Although the majority of these traders work in offices managed and maintained by their direct access brokers, a small percentage trades remotely from home, usually via a "private network connection" provided by their direct access broker, says Lee. Either way, he emphasizes, this segment of the population does not include the casual online trader who is trading through traditional online services such as Ameritrade.

Keeping this description in mind, Lee says that the ETA recently conducted "an informal survey" that showed that most direct access traders actually lose money during their first 6 months on the job. During this 6-month period, he says, the losses range from $25,000 to $50,000.

However, Lee emphasizes that the survey—in which the ETA polled a group of large day-trading firms—also showed that two-thirds of the traders who trade beyond this 6-month learning curve become profitable. Moreover, he says, the top one-third of this group becomes very profitable. "The fallacy out there is that all [direct access traders] lose, and nobody can make it. That's just made up out of whole cloth. It has no basis in actual results," says Lee.

Nevertheless, Lee also cautions that in order to make it to the upside, you must be able to put up the risk capital you need to afford the initial down cycle. "There is a very steep learning curve, and people should understand that the majority of people who start in this business lose money. . . . So you have to go in with risk capital, you have to be able to go 6 months without income, and you have to be able to be patient through a pretty steep learning curve," he says.

Indeed, patience enabled Peter Sweeney, a direct access trader, to survive his rough initiation into the world of direct access trading. "The first 6 months I lost my . . . [butt] because I traded too much. I almost busted out, but then I made it all back in the next 6 months," he says.

Besides great patience, Sweeney says, he had the financial and emotional resolve that he needed to make it through the tough times. "That's why so many of the . . . [direct access traders] bust out—because they are not prepared financially or emotionally to lose," he says.

Unfortunately, the exact percentage of direct access traders who quit remains unclear. Lee has no specific figure for the number of traders who fail but says that when you are measuring success, it is important to divide direct access traders into two camps—"people in the learning curve and people out of the learning curve." Clearly, he says, if you have only been trading for 4 months as opposed to, say, 3 years, then it is likely that you will not be nearly as profitable as your more experienced colleagues.

However, Lee cannot pinpoint the primary reason why some traders make it beyond the 6-month learning curve and some do not. "People can't be pigeonholed. It's like saying, 'Why can't voters make up their mind about the presidential election?' There are too many factors going into this right now," he says.

One of the "factors" that everyone trading stocks in the United States should consider is the division between *informed order flow* and *uninformed order flow,* says Tradescape.com's Omar Amanat. These two types of order flow, says Amanat, separate electronic communication networks (ECNs), direct access brokers, and direct access traders from market makers, online discount brokers, and their clients.

Informed order flow, which seeks the best price and fastest execution, is the playground of the former group. Uninformed order flow, which is "not necessarily time- and price-sensitive," is the domain of the latter group, says Amanat.

Uninformed order flow, of course, includes the payment for order flow (PFOF) arrangements we have already discussed in great detail. Unfortunately, Amanat says that even in the wake of decimalization, he is not sure how fast these PFOF agreements are going to end. Today, he says, too many online discount brokers are still concerned mainly with maximizing their order flow assets. "Some brokers make $50 million a year in order flow, and they're not going to necessarily give that up right away. They'd rather continue to send that order flow to market makers," says Amanat.

In contrast, direct access brokers are leaving the power to find the best execution and best price for a stock in the hands of their direct access trading customers. These traders, in turn, usually are seeking the best trades. "It's kind of a bit of an irony that we call day trading order flow informed order flow. But in fact, because it is time- and price-sensitive, that's the difference. You're really trying to get the fastest, best possible execution for yourself," Amanat says.

FUTURE LOOKS DIRECT

As he gazes into his crystal ball, ETA's Lee predicts that—thanks to such perks as better execution and price improvement—more and more stock traders are going to migrate to direct access technology in the near future. Currently, Lee says that the average direct access trader trades between 35,000 and 50,000 shares a day—at a clip of around 450 shares per trade. Typically, he says, these traders are entering orders to buy or sell a stock in 1000-share lots but—due to various market conditions—usually are getting partial fills.

Lee thinks that the aggregate number of shares direct access traders trade per day likely will increase, but he contends that there is definitely room for direct access technology to grow within the active online trading community.

Indeed, direct access technology is already begging to spread its wings among Watcher Technologies' community of traders. Today, many of the firm's direct access clients are executing between 50 and 200 trades per day, says Watcher Technologies' President Paul Hindes. Gradually, however, Watcher's system has made inroads among a group of online traders who are making 10 to 20 trades per day—a sector of the market that historically has used standard online brokerage technology.

However, Hindes also says that Watcher's system, in its current incarnation, is definitely not designed for the 3 trades per month investor. "The 10 trades per day person is certainly going to move toward direct access trading," he says. "[But] I don't think we're going to see a regular old individual investor doing direct access trading. It's quite complicated, and just to read level II quotes is an art in itself."

ProTrader's Jon Bunda, meanwhile, says that because direct access technology reduces the "overall costs of trading" and eliminates unnecessary intermediaries, its migration toward the mainstream is inevitable. It just makes much more economic sense, he says, to execute a trade directly rather than by emailing your order to an online broker who, in turn, routes that order to a market maker. "Removing those steps along the way, where someone else earns a commission on the transactions, has to make the whole trading process more efficient. If I'm accessing the market directly, that's a lot different than if two or three people touch my order by the time it gets executed," he says. "So the trend is toward more and more direct access for everybody. That has nothing to do with direct access being inherently good or bad, other than the fact that it's more efficient."

Tradescape's Scott Ignall agrees but cautions that direct access trading is not for everyone. If you are a really inexperienced trader, he says, direct access technology can be dangerous because it yields complete control of the trade to the trader. "It leaves the trade at your discretion as far as price and time are concerned, . . . so it could turn into a bit of a poison for an inexperienced trader," he says.

However, Ignall also says that if an active, experienced trader wants total control of an order and is "serious about getting the best possible execution price for a stock," then direct access trading is the only way to go. For the serious trader, he says, direct access technology provides many advantages—including the power to see all the underlying bids and offers for a stock and the ability to act as a de facto market maker.

However, some industry observers believe that direct access technology is suitable for all types of investors. For example, All-Tech's Harvey Houtkin says that regardless of your level of trading experience, direct access trading "eliminates the scum in the middle" and therefore is your best possible option for stock trading. "I don't care whether you're holding a stock for a minute and flipping it or holding it for a week or 10 years. It doesn't make a difference. [Direct access trading] . . . represents the best execution, and you want to get the best price for a stock regardless of how long you're going to hold it," he says.

Using a traditional online brokerage system instead of a direct access system, says Houtkin, is analogous to riding on a "beaten up old bicycle" in lieu of driving a big luxury car. "Anyone who trades at all should be using direct access equipment. If you're not using direct access equipment, it just means that you are trading very ineffectually and very stupidly," he says.

This may be a bit of an extremist point of view, but Houtkin's point is clear. Any way you slice it, for traders who want to squeeze the best price and fastest execution out of each and every trade they make, direct access technology is the premier option.

Similarly, if you are willing to put in the time it takes to get educated and gain experience, direct access trading offers you the most lucrative venue for buying and selling stocks. However, whether you choose to become a scalper, a momentum player, or a position trader, you must diligently build your knowledge of Nasdaq level II. Once you learn the intricacies of level II, you will be better equipped to read and analyze the moves of market makers who trade the stocks you trade. And once you are skilled enough to predict the directions specific market makers are going to take their stocks, you will be on the road to success.

As you evolve, you must devise a trading plan that complements both your personality and your trading capital. And perhaps more significantly, you must implement a risk-management scheme that gives you the discipline you need to get out of a position before your losses mount. For some people, a simple mental stop loss is the only discipline they need to curtail risk. For others, successful risk management may require the use of additional strategies—such as reducing share size when losses mount.

Remember, the object, at least at first, is to stay in the game. Then, after you have survived that initial rush, you can set your sights on maximizing your profits.

Of course, no matter which strategy you employ, there is no guarantee that you are going to make loads of money. However, whether you are in the red or the black, you would be wise to always stay within your profit and loss parameters. Do not forget: A fool and his (or her) money are soon parted.

GLOSSARY

Accumulation   A sideways market at the bottom of the cycle where Wall Street insiders and the smart money are accumulating stock in anticipation of an impending rally.

Advance-decline (A/D) line   The daily sum of the total number of stocks that went up in price less the total number of stocks that went down in price. The A/D line should move with the market to confirm its direction. If it diverges, the market is thought to be on the verge of a reversal.

All or none   An order to purchase or sell a security in which the broker/ dealer is instructed to fill the entire order or not to fill it at all.

Analyst   An individual employed by large brokerage firms who analyzes the fundamentals of a company and issues earnings expectations and other information relating to the company's stock.

Arbitrage   A transaction in which, given that the same security is selling at two different prices, a security is bought at the lower price and resold at the higher price.

Ask price   The price at which market participants offer to sell a security.

Auction market   A market such as the New York Stock Exchange, where trading occurs in one place and a specialist makes markets and provides liquidity.

Bar chart   A chart that shows the high and low prices of the day for a stock as a long stick or bar. The horizontal peg attached to the side of the bar indicates the closing price.

Basis point   A measure of interest rates, where one basis point is $1/100$ of 1 percent.

Bear   A trader who expects market prices to decline. A trader can also be described as *bearish*.

Bear market   A market with declining prices.

Bid price   The price at which market participants offer to buy a security.

Bond   An investment instrument in which the seller of the bond agrees to pay back the price of the bond as well as a premium.

Bollinger bands   Lines drawn above and below a primary trend line that indicate a confidence region within which price should stay. The distance between a Bollinger band and the estimated primary trend line is calculated on the basis of the estimated standard deviations of the stock price.

Breakout   When price moves above the resistance level or below the support level. A good sign for a breakout is that there is heavy volume accompanying it.

Broker   A financial intermediary who brings buyers and sellers together and charges commissions.

Bull   A trader who expects market prices to increase.

Bull market   A market with increasing prices.

Calendar effects   These are effects relating to the time of year, quarter, month, or even day. For example, it is a stylized fact that stocks seem to do better in January. Also known as *seasonal effects*.

Cheap talk   A term that refers to the ability to send out signals costlessly; e.g., a threat to veto a bill by the President is considered cheap talk.

Commission   The charge that a broker collects for serving as the intermediary in a financial transaction.

Consolidation pattern   See *Continuation pattern.*

Continuation pattern   This is a pattern that forms as a sideways market in the middle of a rally or a decline. The stock has stopped to catch its breath, so to speak. Also known as *consolidation pattern.*

Correction   A term referring to a fall in the market of less than 20 percent.

Coupon   The interest that is paid to a bondholder for a bond.

Day order   An order that is specified to be filled within the day it is placed or else canceled.

Day trader   A trader who closes out all positions at the end of the day for cash.

Dealer-driven market   A market, such as the Nasdaq, where multiple market makers compete against each other as providers of liquidity.

Distribution   A pattern that forms as a rectangle at market tops where Wall Street insiders and informed investors are said to be distributing stock to uninformed investors in anticipation of an impending fall in the stock price.

Downbid   A decrease of one level in the price of a stock on the Nasdaq.

Downtick   A decrease in the price of a stock on the New York Stock Exchange of one level, in which a trade has taken place.

Electronic Communication Networks (ECNs)   The virtual markets where Nasdaq stocks trade.

Envelopes   Lines that are drawn parallel to an estimated trend line at some fixed distance from the stock price. These lines often are used as indicators that the stock is making a large move if the price wanders past one of them. See also *Bollinger bands.*

Equity   Ownership in a firm, e.g., by ownership of stock issued by a firm.

Fundamental analysis   Analyzing the potential changes in the price of a stock based on the company's fundamentals, such as the P/E ratio, debt ratio, and so on.

Fundamentals   Information relating to a company that is used to predict the success and profitability of the company by some market participants. Some fundamentals may be debt ratio, market share, etc.

Gap When a stock price opens at a different price than it closed the previous day.

Good-till-canceled An order with a restriction that stipulates that the order is in effect until canceled.

Index fund A mutual fund whose basket of stocks is the same as the basket used by some market index of securities.

Institutional investor A term used to refer to firms that invest in the stock market, instead of individuals.

Inside market The best prices available for trading, the highest bid and the lowest ask.

Leverage A term referring to debt, often used to describe how much of an investment or position is financed by borrowing.

Limit order An order to be filled only at a price no worse than a specified price level, called the *limit price.*

Liquidity The ability to enter/exit an investment or make a transaction quickly and at low costs because there are buyers and sellers willing to take opposite position.

Listed stocks Stocks sold on the New York Stock Exchange.

Long position When an investor owns a stock in anticipation of a price increase. Selling stock that one owns is called a *long sale.*

Marker maker A market participant responsible for providing liquidity, i.e., who stands ready to buy or sell from traders.

Market order An order to be filled immediately as it is placed and at the current market prices.

Market risk The risk that the value of any one stock will be affected by the general value of other assets on the market.

Money market The market for securities with short-term maturity, usually less than 1 year.

Mutual fund A company that invests the aggregate money of its shareholders in the markets.

NASD National Association of Securities Dealers. The organization whose member firms make markets in the Nasdaq markets.

NYSE New York Stock Exchange.

Offer The price at which a market maker offers to sell a stock.

Open outcry   The system of trading stocks in which individuals gather around a prespecified trading area and shout out the bids and offers.

Order flow   A term referring to the stream of buying amounts that are observed by, for example, a specialist on the New York Stock Exchange. Another example would be large brokerage firms who observe internal order flow from their clients.

Over-the-counter   A market for securities in which trading occurs off an organized exchange, among brokers and investors.

Penetration   When the price moves beyond a resistance or support line or some other boundary implied by technical analysis as having the effect of signaling a potential change in the underlying primary trend. See also *Breakout.*

Primary market   The market for securities when they are offered initially to the public and have not been traded previously.

Primary trend   The trend that is said to be governing the general movement of a stock price in the long run. This trend captures the general direction of the stock price over long periods of time.

Profit taking   When a sell-off of some stock ensues because investors feel that the price is high and they want cash instead of the stock.

Pure discount bond   A bond such as a Treasury bill that pays no coupon but sells at a discount from its par value.

Quote   The description of the market for a stock, which includes bid and ask prices, as well as the size of the quantities supplied and demanded at those prices.

Rally   When the price of a stock steadily increases.

Rectangle   A pattern of price movement in which the price bounces back and forth from a support to a resistance level, and these support and resistance lines are parallel to each other. Hence the price movement forms a rectangle. Also known as a *sideways market.*

Resistance   A price level that represents a psychological barrier for the market beyond which the price of a stock cannot rise. Often, when a stock reaches the resistance level, investors fear that the price will fall, as it has before, and sell, which causes the price to fall.

Return   The increase in wealth (often measured as a percent) due to investing in some asset.

Reversal   When a trend, especially the primary trend, changes direction and the stock moves the other way.

Risk-free rate   The return of an asset with no risk.

Risk premium   The return above the risk-free rate that investors demand for assuming some asset risk.

Scalper   A trader who derives profits from holding assets just long enough to exploit arbitrage opportunities that arise from small price changes.

Secondary market   The market for assets that were issued previously and trade among investors.

Secondary trend   Short-term fluctuations in price that wrap themselves around the primary trend. These are movements in price that have no consequence for the long-term position of the price.

Sell-off   When a large number of shares are offered in the market for a stock, causing its price to fall.

Short position   When an investor sells a stock short.

Short sale   A sale of an asset that is borrowed from a broker and later purchased from the market and returned to the broker. The idea of a short sale is to borrow stock to sell while the price is high and later buy it back to replace the borrowed stock when the price is low.

SOES   Small Order Execution System.

Specialist   The individual who is in charge of making markets and providing liquidity for stocks traded on the New York Stock Exchange.

Spread   The difference between the bid price and the ask price.

Stock index   A measure of the performance of a stock market or some sector of the stock market consisting of an averaging of some or all the stocks traded in the market or sector.

Stop order   An order that calls for the transaction to be filled until the stock price reaches the stop price.

Support   A price level that represents a psychological barrier for the market beyond which the price of a stock cannot fall. Often, when a stock reaches the support level, investors assume that the price will increase, as it has before, and buy, which causes the price to increase.

Technical analysis   Analyzing the behavior of stock price movements over time by way of stock price charts and graphs.

Upbid   An increase in the price of a stock on the Nasdaq of one level.

Uptick   An increase in the price of a stock on the New York Stock Exchange of one level, in which a trade has taken place.

Whipsaw   A temporary change in direction of the price when it is following a general trend. A whipsaw occurs when the price of a stock crosses over a moving-average line, for example, and then crosses back later on and continues its previous trend.

Yield   The discount rate for a bond, which equates the present value of the coupons paid by the bond and the principal to the price.

Zero-plus tick   When a trade takes place on the New York Stock Exchange for some stock in which price has not changed, but in the previous change, price had increased.

INDEX

ABOUT THE AUTHOR

Robert Sales is editor of *Electronic Trading Week*, a newsletter that covers all facets of automated trading at financial services firms. A senior editor and editorial chief of trading systems supplements for *Wall Street and Technology* magazine, Sales has served as both a speaker and a moderator on a number of electronic trading panels.